THE INVESTOR'S
GUIDEBOOK TO

FIXED INCOME
INVESTMENTS

THE INVESTOR'S GUIDEBOOK TO

FIXED INCOME INVESTMENTS

Bond Markets—A Handbook
for Issuers and Investors

STUART R. VEALE

Prentice Hall Press

PRENTICE HALL PRESS
Published by the Penguin Group
Penguin Group (USA) LLC
375 Hudson Street, New York, New York 10014

USA • Canada • UK • Ireland • Australia • New Zealand • India • South Africa • China

penguin.com

A Penguin Random House Company

Library of Congress Cataloging-in-Publication Data

Veale, Stuart R.
The investor's guidebook to fixed income investments: bond markets: a handbook
for issuers and investors / Stuart R. Veale.
pages   cm
Includes index.
ISBN 978-0-7352-0531-4 (pbk)
1. Finance, Personal.   2. Investments.   3. Bonds.   4. Options (Finance)   I. Title.
HG179.V43   2013
332.63'23   2013032623

First edition: December 2013

PRINTED IN THE UNITED STATES OF AMERICA

10 9 8 7 6 5 4 3 2

This book is dedicated to:

the thousands of sales and trading, banking, capital markets, compliance, and middle market analysts and associates I have had the pleasure of teaching over the last 25 years. It was my pleasure to help launch your careers and watch you rise to assuming leadership positions thoughout the industry.

ACKNOWLEDGMENTS

Though a book has one author, it has countless contributors. In particular, I'd like to acknowledge the contribution of Goldman Sachs and Morgan Stanley Smith Barney Inc. new hires for refining the way the information in this book is presented. I'd also like to thank my editor at Penguin Group, Jeanette Shaw, and her staff for their patience and professionalism in shepherding this project from vision to completion.

CONTENTS

FOREWORD

I finished the second edition of my book on investing called *Stocks, Bonds, Options, Futures (SBOF)* in 2001. Here we are 12 years later. While the second edition was still selling well, it was also overdue for an update. Over the last 12 years, much has changed in the way stocks and bonds were priced, traded, analyzed, packaged, and marketed. Specialists on the New York Stock Exchange were replaced with designated market makers. The volume of trades executed on the dark pools soared. Derivatives on rainfall and wind had become hot products. Twenty-four-hour trading became a reality. The variety of exotic options exploded. Exchange-traded funds became the fastest growing financial product in history, etc.

I started out to write the third edition of *SBOF*, but it quickly became clear the industry had become too broad and too complex to comfortably fit in one text. Therefore, after discussing it with my publisher and readers, I made the decision to break the book into four manageable volumes:

- *The Investor's Guidebook to Derivatives*
- *The Investor's Guidebook to Alternative Investments*

- *The Investor's Guidebook to Fixed Income Investments*
- *The Investor's Guidebook to Equities*

My hope is that by expanding the book into four volumes, I'll be able to make them more comprehensive, include more examples, and make the books more useful to my readers. While I made every effort to proof the text, there will undoubtedly be errors for which I assume full responsibility. It is my intent to update these volumes frequently, and therefore, I welcome my readers' suggestions on which topics should be added, expanded, and omitted in future editions. Please email your questions, critiques, and comments to stu@invest-perform.com. I hope to answer every email I receive.

This book was prepared from sources believed to be reliable but which are not guaranteed. The research analyst who is primarily responsible for this research and whose name is listed on the front cover certifies that: (1) all of the views expressed in this research accurately reflect his personal views about any and all of the subject securities or issuers; and (2) no part of any of the research analyst's compensation was, is, or will be directly or indirectly related to the specific recommendations or views expressed by the research analyst. Opinions and estimates constitute my judgment as of this writing and are subject to change without notice. Past performance is not indicative of future results. This material is not intended as an offer or solicitation for the purchase or sale of any financial instrument. Securities, financial instruments, or strategies mentioned herein may not be suitable for all investors. The opinions and recommendations herein do not take into account individual client circumstances, objectives, or needs and are not intended as recommendations of particular securities, financial instruments, or strategies to particular clients. The reader must make independent decisions regarding any securities or financial instruments mentioned herein.

Bonds and other fixed income investments used to be the boring part of most investors' portfolios. They provided the safe foundation on which the riskier investments, like equities, commodities, artwork, derivatives, jewels, and other investments, could rest. No more. Alice has gone through the looking glass. The debt of Western governments, which was once the safest investment in the world, has become highly speculative. We live in a world which is floating on a sea of debt that can't be repaid except by the wholesale printing of money. Thirty years ago, people traded stocks and held debt. Today, many experienced investors believe it is wiser to do the reverse.

This book tries to equip its readers with the concepts they will need to understand to be successful in today's more challenging fixed income market, including:

- Why index selection is probably the most important part of selecting a floating rate note
- Why the call date of convertible bonds is so important

- Why investors must compare the relative return of bonds with different compounding frequencies and calendar conventions
- Why it often makes sense to avoid bonds with high yields to maturity (YTM)
- Why YTM is such a poor metric of true return
- Why some investors have no exposure to inflation
- Why bonds with the same credit ratings and same maturities should offer different YTMs
- Why the total spread and credit spread are very different

In addition to those concepts, this book presents numerous tools, including:

- Using advanced yield measures that incorporate taxes, reinvestment, and/or inflation to maximize horizon analysis
- Using duration to find the trade-off point between interest risk and reinvestment risk
- Using modified duration to measure interest rate risk
- Using convexity to measure volatility risk
- Stacking the deck by riding the yield curve
- Constructing immunized and dedicated portfolios
- Valuing embedded options
- Determining if a bond's credit spread provides adequate compensation for the risk

What this book omits are basic markets stats such as the size of the US Treasury market or the historic yield range for US corporates. These stats constantly change and are readily available on the web, so I saw no reason to waste book space on them.

CHAPTER ONE

Introduction to the Debt Market

What defines the debt market is that in each transaction there is an entity that borrows money (the issuer) and a lender(s) who loans it (investors). The amount of money the lender(s) provide the borrower is called the principal. The borrower uses the money it borrows to buy assets, grow a business, pay its bills, and so forth. Usually, the borrower pays the lender interest (a percentage of the money borrowed) periodically for the use of the money. The rate of interest and the interest payment schedule are determined by negotiation between the borrower and the lenders. When a loan matures (comes due), the borrower returns the principal and any remaining unpaid interest to the lender.

The global debt market (measured as if all debt was first converted to US$) is greater than $200 trillion, which dwarfs the size of the global equity (stock) market. From a purely economic point of view, the debt market is far more important than the equity market.

SEGMENTATION BASED ON MATURITY

The debt market is divided into three segments based upon the time until the loan matures:

- The money market includes loans that mature in 1 year or less.
- The note market includes loans that mature in 1–10 years.
- The bond market includes loans that mature in more than 10 years.

Investors refer to these as 7-year US Treasury note, the 5-year US Treasury note, and the 20-year Treasury bond.

INTEREST PAYMENT FREQUENCY

The frequency of interest payments varies depending upon the type of loan vehicle:

- Daily—money market funds
- Monthly—mortgages
- Quarterly—interest rate swaps
- Semiannual—US notes and bonds
- Annual—euro notes and bonds

THE COUPON

The interest rate (aka the coupon) on the loan can be:

- Fixed for the life of the loan. If the principal is $1,000 and the coupon is 6%, the borrower will pay the investor $60 a year until the principal is repaid. (Note that the interest is always calculated on the face value or principal value of the loan—not the loan's resale value in the secondary market.) Some of the many factors that determine the interest rate on a fixed rate loan include:
  - The current level of interest rates in the market
  - The length of the loan—usually the longer the loan, the higher the rate
  - The credit quality of the borrower
  - The promises the lender makes the investors in exchange for receiving the loan, called covenants. Each covenant is designed to protect the investor's interests. Some examples of these include limitations on:
    - Adding additional debt
    - Selling or disposing of collateral
    - Changing the company's corporate structure
    - Making dividend payments to shareholders or executing stock buyback programs
    - Moving the company to a new country or state
    - Making significant acquisitions
- Tied to an interest rate and allowed to float with that rate. The most commonly used index rates in the US are listed in Figure 1.1.

FIGURE 1.1

Common Floating Rate Indices

Name	Definition
T-bill	The rate at which the US government can borrow money for the short term
LIBOR	The rate at which money center banks lend each other money
COFI	The bank's average cost of funding itself
Prime	The rate the bank charges its best customers to borrow money

Many investors consider the floating rate note (FRN) market to be boring and homogenous. Nothing could be further from the truth. Consider the below situation. XYZ Inc., an industrial firm, has issued two different FRNs with the coupons listed in Figure 1.2.

FIGURE 1.2

Alternative XYZ FRNs Before Crash

Name	Index Rate	Spread	Yield
$6M T-bill	3%	3%	6%
$6M LIBOR	4%	2%	6%

Both notes have equal credit quality, liquidity, and payment dates. As both notes currently yield 6%, how should an investor decide which to buy? The T-bill rate is the rate at which the US government can borrow money, while the LIBOR (London Inter-bank Offering Rate) is the rate at which large money center banks around the world can borrow US dollars. Because banks have more risk than the US government, the LIBOR rate is higher than the T-bill rate. The spread between them is a credit spread—currently

1%—that varies over time. For example, in 2007 there was a flight to quality as it appeared that many banks would collapse. The T-bill rate went to 0, while LIBOR rose to 6%—widening the T-bill/LIBOR spread to 6%. With the spread at 6%, the two notes had the yields listed in Figure 1.3.

FIGURE 1.3

Alternative XYZ FRNs During Crash

Name	Index Rate	Spread	Yield
$6M T-bills	0%	3%	3%
$6M LIBOR	6%	2%	8%

An investor clearly would have been better off buying the note tied to LIBOR and having the yield go from 6% to 8% instead of the T-bill-linked note that went from 6% to 3%. Naturally, after the yield change, the LIBOR note would trade at a premium and the T-bill note would trade at a discount.

The second issue with FRNs is how the formula is quoted. Look at the example shown in Figure 1.4.

FIGURE 1.4

Alternative XYZ FRNs During Crash

Name	Index Rate	Spread	Yield
$6M T-bill	4%	Add 1%	5%
$6M T-bill	4%	125% of Index	5%

The notes are identical with the exception of how the spread is defined. While both notes have an equal return now, the first note will outperform if rates decline, while the second will outperform if rates rise. Even though these are both FRNs, the irony is that investors still need to have an outlook on rates in order in order make the right choice:

- Zero coupon bonds (ZCBs). A ZCB doesn't make periodic interest payments. Instead, the bond is sold at a discount and the payments are compounded internally until the bond matures and it pays its par value to the investor.
- Bonds tied to the price of a commodity or economic indicator. For example the interest you get paid might equal the:
  - Rate of inflation + 1%
  - Percentage increase in the price of oil on the NYMEX over a set time period
  - Difference between the change in the value of the pound and the change in the value of the euro.

MATURITY OF DEBT

The maturity of the loan can be:

- **Fixed (aka a Bullet Loan)**—Neither the issuer nor the investor can alter the life of the loan.
- **Extendable**—The loan has a scheduled maturity date; however, the borrower can elect to extend the term of the loan, usually by paying a previously agreed upon higher interest rate. For example, a typical extendable loan might start as a 10-year 5% loan. If the borrower extends the maturity by 1 year, the rate in year 11 rises to 6%. If the borrower further extends the maturity by an additional year, the rate in year 12 rises to 7%. Finally, the borrower may extend the maturity a third year, but the rate changes to 8%. After 13 years, the

loan is absolutely due. If the principal isn't repaid, the loan is in default.

Extendable loans are most commonly used in the commercial real estate market. For example, a real estate investor buys a building for $10.5MM by putting up $500K and borrowing $10MM for 10 years at 5% with an interest-only mortgage. The investor hopes that the value of the building will rise over the next 10 years, so it can be sold at a profit. If it is sold at a profit, the investor then pays off the mortgage and banks the profit. But suppose in 10 years, the building is only worth $9.7MM. The building can either be sold at a loss—(the investor can put up another $300K to get out of the deal), or the investor can extend the financing. Since the building is worth less than the mortgage, the property can't be refinanced. Instead, the existing loan must be extended for 1–3 years. Hopefully, for the investor, the value of the property will rise to more than $10MM over the next 1–3 years so the investor can refinance.

- **Subject to a Put Option**—If the loan is subject to a put option, the investor has the right to shorten the life of the loan, usually without paying a penalty. The investor can use the put to force the issuer to repurchase the bond at par—regardless of its current market value. The borrower will exercise the option if interest rates rise (so the investor can reinvest the principal at a higher rate) or if the issuer's credit quality declines. Put options have three variables:
  - *Period of Put Protection*—This is the period of time that passes between when the note is issued before the put option is activated or "knocked-in." For example, a 10-year note might have 3 years of put protection meaning that the put option is only activated 3 years after the note was issued. A 20-year bond might have 5 years of "put protection."

- *Life of the Option*—Once the option is knocked-in, three things can happen:
  - › The option can stay activated for the remaining life of the note. In this case the investor can put the bond any business day.
  - › The option can stay active for a brief period (a week or a month) and then turn off. This is a "use it or lose it" option. If the investor does not use the put during this period, the option is lost. If a 10-year note has a 3-year use it or lose it option, and the option is not used, the investor is left with 7-year bullet paper.
  - › The option can turn on and off, and then turn on again later on. For example, the 10-year note may become putable on its 3-year, 5-year and 7-year anniversary.
- *Hard or Soft Put*—A put can be "hard" or "soft." If the put is "soft" the put can only be activated if some additional condition is met beyond passing the period of put protection. For example, one or more of the following conditions may have to be true in order for the put option to be activated:
  - › The credit quality of the issuer is downgraded.
  - › Management changes.
  - › The bond's secondary market value drops below some pre-specified value.
- **Subject to a Call Option**—A note/bond can also have an embedded call option. If the loan is callable, the issuer has the right to shorten the loan. The issuer will exercise (use) this option when rates have declined so that the issuer can stop paying a high interest rate and reissue debt at a lower interest rate. Embedded call options have the same three variables as put options, namely:
  - A period of call protection.

- Three alternatives once the option is activated.
- The option can be hard or soft.

However, unlike puts, call options also have an additional variable—the call premium. When the issuer calls a bond, the reason is that interest rates have declined since the bond was issued and it can issue new bonds at a lower rate. For example, a company might issue a 10% 20-year bond that is callable in 5 years. If, in 5 years, interest rates are at 6%, the issuer will no longer want to pay 10% and so will call in the 10% bond issue. The investor will then receive their money back and have to reinvest it at a lower rate. Because calls always hurt investors, most issuers try to partially offset the pain by calling the bond at a premium to par. This premium price is still less than the bond's true value—but at least it is a gesture of goodwill. A typical premium schedule for a 20-year bond with 5 years of call projection would be:
- $1,040 if the bond is called in year 6.
- $1,030 if the bond is called in year 7.
- $1,020 if the bond is called in year 8.
- $1,010 if the bond is called in year 9.
- $1,000 if the bond is called in year 10 or later.

Note: It costs money to call in a bond and issue new ones and so the interest savings must at least cover the costs. Therefore, if the company is paying 10% and interest rates for new bonds drop to 9.97%, the issuer will not call in its 10% bonds.
- **Subject to a Sinking Fund**—If a bond is subject to a sinking fund, the issuer is required to periodically pay off a portion of the principal instead of paying it off all at once at maturity.

For example, suppose a company issues $100MM of 8% 10-year notes to raise the money to build a new factory. The notes, however, are subject to the sinking fund in Figure 1.5.

FIGURE 1.5

Cash Flow Schedule for a Sinking Bond

Year	Interest	Amount Retired End of Year	Total Cash Flow	Remaining Debt
1	$8,000,000	$0	$8,000,000	$100,000,000
2	$8,000,000	$0	$8,000,000	$100,000,000
3	$8,000,000	$5,000,000	$13,000,000	$95,000,000
4	$7,600,000	$5,000,000	$12,600,000	$90,000,000
5	$7,200,000	$5,000,000	$12,200,000	$85,000,000
6	$6,800,000	$5,000,000	$11,800,000	$80,000,000
7	$6,400,000	$7,500,000	$13,900,000	$72,500,000
8	$5,800,000	$7,500,000	$13,300,000	$65,000,000
9	$5,200,000	$7,500,000	$12,700,000	$57,500,000
10	$4,600,000	$57,500,000	$62,100,000	$0

From an operational perspective, prior to the annual anniversary of the issue, the issuer can either:

- Buy back the required number of bonds in the open market if the bonds are trading below par in the secondary market. After it buys them back, it cancels them.
- Call in the bonds (usually by random draw) if the bonds are trading above par in the secondary market.

A well-designed sinking fund benefits both the issuer and investors. Looking at the schedule shown in Figure 1.5, in years 1 and 2, the plant is being built and debugged, and so it is not generating any cash. The borrower is only paying the interest to keep its cash flow requirements to a minimum. By year 3, however, the plant should be running flat out and generating a profit. The issuer can use that profit to pay down some of its debt and therefore lower its future interest expense.

From the investor's point of view, as the plant generates profits, using those profits to pay down the principal reduces the investor's credit risk. At the end of year 10, the borrower only needs to pay off or refinance $57.5MM instead of $100MM. Even though the plant is now 10 years old, it should still be worth at least $57.5MM.

A targeted redemption note (TARN) is a floating rate note that matures when the investor receives a certain amount of interest. If the total interest amount is 20%, the note will mature in 2 years if interest rates average 10%. The note will mature in 4 years if interest rates average 5%.

CREDIT RATING

Credit risk is the risk that the loan either won't be repaid in full or will be repaid late. Naturally, different loans have different levels of credit risk. Some loans have virtually no risk, such as a short-term loans to the US government. Other loans have a high degree of risk, such as loans to start-up mining operations or biotech companies that haven't yet perfected their products. High-risk loans naturally pay higher interest rates.

Because most investors lack the expertise to assess the level of credit risk in a particular loan, there are companies, such as Moody's and Standard & Poor's, that offer professional credit analysis services. They assign loans ratings based on the probability that the loans will be repaid in full and on time. The ratings range from Aaa/AAA for a bond that has virtually no credit risk down to C or D for bonds that are already in default or where default is a high probability. The table shown in Figure 1.6 explains the major ratings.

FIGURE 1.6

Ratings from Major Rating Agencies

Moody's	Standard & Poor's	Meaning
Aaa	AAA	Highest Credit Quality
Aa	AA	
A	A	
Baa	BBB	Investment Grade
Ba	BB	
B	B	
Caa	C	
C	D	Default or Near Default

CAPITAL STRUCTURE

When corporations issue more than one bond, the relative seniority of each bond becomes a major issue. The seniority of the company's various debt issues is referred to as the company's capital structure. A typical capital structure is as follows:

- Senior debt with no recourse
- Secured debt with recourse
- Bank loans
- Derivative obligations
- Senior unsecured debt
- Trade obligations
- Senior subordinated debt
- Subordinated debt

- Convertible debt
- Income bond
- Preferred stock
- Common stock

Senior Debt with No Recourse

Senior debt with no recourse is secured debt that is not on the company's balance sheet. A typical example would be as follows: A Ba rated US airline wants to borrow $100MM to buy a new aircraft. If the company borrows the money directly, it will have to pay a very high rate of interest because of its low credit rating. Instead, the company creates an independent special purpose corporation (SPC). The SPC is a completely separate entity that raises $20MM in equity plus $80MM in debt for a total of $100MM in capital. Because this debt is fully collateralized by the airplane and has $20MM of equity underneath it, it is priced like Aa rated debt.

The SPC uses its $100MM to buy the plane and then leases the plane to the airline. The airline only pays a monthly lease fee, as shown in Figure 1.7.

FIGURE 1.7

Typical Off Balance Sheet Financing Structure

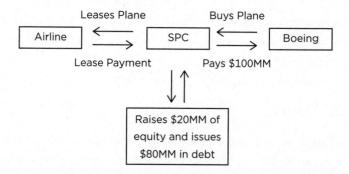

In the event the airline files for bankruptcy, the airline can either:

- Maintain the lease payments, which it probably would do since its newest planes are the most comfortable and fuel efficient.
- Cancel the lease, in which case the SPC can lease the plane to another airline or resell the plane outright.

Since neither the plane nor the SPC is owned by the airline, the bankruptcy court has no jurisdiction over the SPC, its property, or its investors. This is what is meant by "no recourse."

Secured Debt with Recourse

An alternative way for the airline to lower its financing costs is to issue the debt directly—but then secure the debt with segregated collateral. For example, the airline could buy the plane directly in its own name, and then put collateral (such as the title to the aircraft) into a trust account that was earmarked to serve as collateral just for this debt issue. Only after all the debt was paid off would any remaining value be available to other creditors. As long as the value of the plane exceeds the size of the debt, the debt is fully collateralized. Thus, the debt needs to be paid down at a faster rate than the airplane depreciates. In the event the company goes bankrupt, the investors will have to go through the bankruptcy process to pursue their claim.

Bank Loans

The first level of unsecured debt is bank lines of credit. Most companies maintain lines of credit that they can draw against to meet short-term cash shortfalls. These lines of credit are usually the most senior unsecured debt on the balance sheet. The term unsecured means that no collateral is specifically escrowed or segregated to back the debt. However, just because the debt doesn't have segregated assets backing it, doesn't mean the company doesn't have sufficient assets to secure the debt. The company may have assets whose value is thousands of times greater than the company's debts, but the assets are not specifically segregated to guarantee the debt.

Derivative Obligations

If the company has entered into any derivative contracts, such as interest rate swaps, cross currency swaps, and the like, these obligations are usually very senior. They must be paid before interest is paid to any debt that does not have specific collateral escrowed for its protection.

Senior Unsecured Debt

Just like bank debt, the senior unsecured debt might or might not have assets behind it. However, if it does, the assets are not segregated or escrowed. A company can have multiple debt issues at each level of the capital structure. Debt issues with the same seniority are said to be *pari passu*. Debt issues that are *pari passu* can be issued at different times and even be denominated in different currencies.

Trade Obligations

Trade obligations include vendors who provide products and services to the company and then send a bill—normally payable in

30 days. Examples of trade obligations include legal fees, accounting fees, other consultants, office supply stores, food vendors, custodian services, and the like. These bills are junior to the senior debt.

Subordinated Debt

The term "subordinated debt" means the debt is junior to the senior debt and is either *pari passu* with or subordinate to trade obligations. A company can have multiple levels of subordinated debt ranging from senior subordinate to junior subordinate. Subordinate debt almost never has specific collateral escrowed for its protection. Bonds without escrowed collateral are sometimes referred to as debentures.

Convertible Bonds

A convertible security is a debt-equity hybrid that contains an embedded option that grants the investor the right to exchange the security for another type of security. While there are innumerable varieties of convertible securities, the most traditional and common types of convertible securities are bonds and preferred stocks that investors can exchange for a fixed number of shares of the company's common stock.

Consider a bond issued by XYZ Inc. This bond is issued at par with a 6% coupon and includes an option that allows the bond to be converted at any time into 100 shares of a company's common stock. At the time the bond is issued, the company's common is selling for $8 per share and pays no dividend.

No rational investor would buy the bond and immediately exchange it for the stock since the $1,000 bond could only be exchanged for $800 worth of stock (100 shares × $8 per share). However, if a year later the stock is selling for $16 per share, the bond can be converted into $1,600 worth of stock. If the bond was selling at any price below $1,600, an investor could make an immediate risk free (arbitrage) profit by buying the bond, exchanging it for stock, and selling the stock.

In reality, the bond would be worth more than $1,600 because, in addition to being convertible into $1,600 worth of the company's common stock, it also generates $60 of income per year for its owner. The present value of those future interest payments would have to be added to the conversion value in order to determine the bond's fair current market value. Before we discuss convertible securities in more detail, it is necessary to become familiar with several terms and ratios related to convertible securities.

Conversion Value

The conversion value is the current market value of the common stock into which the bond converts. It is calculated by multiplying the number of shares into which the bond converts by the current price of the common stock.

Conversion value = number shares × price of the shares

In the XYZ Inc. bond example, the initial conversion value would be:

Conversion value = 100 × $8 = $800

After the stock rose to $16 per share, the conversion value would be:

Conversion value = 100 × $16 = $1,600

Conversion Premium

The conversion premium is the difference between the market value and the conversion value of the bond—expressed on either an absolute or a percentage basis. In the above example the initial conversion premiums would be:

Absolute premium = $1,000 – $800 = $200
Percentage (aka relative) premium = ($1,000 – $800) /
$800 = 25%

In the United States, the typical initial conversion premium for convertible bonds is 17% to 30%. The initial conversion premium is determined by the perceived upside potential of the stock and the period of call protection. The greater the stock's upside and the longer the period of call protection, the higher the conversion premium investors are willing to pay. The conversion premium declines as the bond approaches its call date (see call risk below) or maturity date.

Work-Out Period

One of the most useful ratios for analysis of convertible bonds is the work-out period. The work-out period is a measure of how long it takes for the conversion premium to be amortized by the higher current income generated by the bond. In the XYZ Inc. bond example, the bond generates current income of $60 per year, while the stock generates no income since it pays no dividends. Since the bond has a $200 conversion premium, the work-out period would be:

$$\text{Work-Out Period} = \frac{\text{Conversion Premium}}{\text{Income from an Equivalent Investment in Stock}}$$

Work-Out Period = $200 / ($60 – $0) = 3.33 years

If the stock generated a $.10 dividend per year, then the work-out period would be:

Work-Out Period = $200 / ($60—$12.50) = 4.21 years

Note that in this example, the income from the stock is $12.50, since $1,000 would buy 125 shares of stock at $8 each. In order to have a fair comparison, it is necessary to compute the work-out period using the income from an equal investment in both the convertible bond and the underlying common.

The shorter the work-out period, the more attractive the convertible is when compared to the underlying stock. Conservative investors are often willing to buy convertibles with work-out periods as long as 3.5 years, while aggressive investors are often unwilling to accept work-out periods longer than 2.5 years.

Why Investors Like Convertibles

Investors always have to choose between the various ways to invest in a company. They can invest directly by buying the common stock or indirectly by buying a security that converts into the common. Convertibles offer investors numerous advantages relative to investing directly in common stock. Some of these advantages of converts versus common stock include:

- **More Senior Security**—In the event the company files for bankruptcy, the investors who own the convertible bonds become creditors of the company and, as such, have a senior claim on any remaining assets relative to both the common and preferred stock holders. Of course, in order for this seniority to have any value, the company has to have assets after the more senior creditors, including the government, employees, vendors, and senior debt holders, are all paid in full.

- **Higher Current Income**—Convertible bonds almost always offer a higher current income than the underlying common stocks. The cash flow from the bond's interest payments almost always exceeds the dividend payments from an equal size investment in the underlying common stock. For investors that require or desire current income, convertibles are often the more attractive investment alternative.

- **Favorable Risk Adjusted Return**—Because of the way that the value of the embedded conversion option changes as the price of the underlying instrument changes, the price of the convertible rises by more when the price of the underlying stock rises than the price of the convertible declines when the underlying stock declines. Thus, convertible securities exhibit a positive asymmetric risk-reward pattern in response to a change in the value of the underlying common.

- **Automatic Tactical Asset Allocation**—One of the most attractive advantages of convertible securities is that they automate one of the most basic and important tactical asset allocation decisions investors have—the decision of how much to allocate to equity versus fixed income. Many market timers try to increase the weighting of stocks in their portfolio when the market is rising and retreat to the higher income and relative safety of bonds when they expect the stock market to decline. Fortunately, for owners of convertible securities, these securities behave more like stocks when the market is rising and more like bonds when the market is either flat or declining. In effect, they automatically tactically reallocate in a way that benefits the investor.

- **Outperforming a Benchmark**—One way of outperforming an equity benchmark is to substitute a carefully selected portfolio of convertible securities for all or part of the benchmark. It is important to note that outperform means outperforming on a risk adjusted basis. A portfolio of convertibles will usually offer a lower total return than a portfolio of common stocks—but it will also have lower risk. If the return of a portfolio of convertibles is 20% lower than the return of a portfolio of common stocks, but the convertibles only have 60% of the risk of the common stocks, the converts offer 80% of the return for 60% of the risk—hence outperforming on a risk adjusted basis.

While convertible securities offer numerous advantages, they also have some disadvantages that investors need to consider.

- **Underperforming the Common**—In a down, flat, or slowly rising market, convertible securities will outperform the underlying common. However, in a rapidly rising market, convertible securities will underperform the underlying common stocks.
- **Call Risk**—Almost every convertible bond is callable. Generally, the bonds are callable either after a certain period of call protection is passed or after the stock price has risen to the point where the conversion option is deeply in the money. When the issuer calls the bond, the investor can lose any remaining conversion premium. Consider the following example:

Suppose the XYZ Inc. bond introduced in the example is purchased as a new issue and that subsequently the underlying stock price rises to $16 a share. Since the conversion value is $1,600 and the bond generates a higher current income, an investor might be willing to pay a $150 premium over conversion value—$1,750 in this example.

However, paying a premium over conversion value can be

a disaster if the bond shortly becomes callable. If the bond is called, the investor would have little choice other than to convert the bond into the underlying common. While converting the bond into $1,600 worth of stock beats accepting $1,000 (or $1,030) in cash from the call, it still results in a loss if the bond was purchased at $1750. When the bond is called, the $150 conversion premium ($1750 − $1600) is lost. Therefore, it is important for investors to research the call provisions of convertible securities prior to purchasing a convertible bond or preferred. Investors should not pay a conversion premium that is higher than the present value of the incremental cash flows the investor can expect to receive from the bond before the bond is called.

- **Loss of Accrued Interest upon Forced Conversion**—When a convertible bond is called, and the investor is effectively forced to convert the bond into the underlying common in order to avoid receiving the call price for the bond, the investor also sacrifices any interest that the bond has accrued. Because they don't have to pay the accrued interest on bonds that are converted, many companies that have issued convertibles often force conversion by calling the securities just prior to an interest payment date.

  Thus, in a forced call an investor can lose both the conversion premium and any accrued interest. Because accrued interest is lost when a convertible is called, it is not uncommon for bonds that are likely to be called to be trading at a price that is equal to their conversion value less their accrued interest.

- **Lower Liquidity of Convertibles**—Convertible securities have lower liquidity than the underlying common. Investors should use limit orders and build orders over time in order to avoid disturbing the market.

Why Do Issuers Issue Converts?

There are four main reasons why issuers elect to issue convertibles:

- To borrow money at a lower rate. By embedding a conversion option into its debt, companies with decent credit ratings can borrow money at a lower interest rate than they would ordinarily have to pay.
- To borrow money at any rate. For start-up companies, or companies with low credit ratings, embedding a conversion option into its bond may be a necessary incentive to attract lenders, even if the bond offers a higher return.
- To unload a block of stock at a favorable price. Suppose a company, ABC, tries to take over another company, DEF, and, despite accumulating 20% of DEF's stock, ABC's takeover fails. Since the takeover failed, DEF's stock price will be depressed. If ABC was to dump its 20% holding onto the market right after the takeover failed, it would only push the price lower. However, the company that acquired the stock can't afford to have capital tied up in this block of stock. The solution is for ABC to issue a convertible note that converts into the DEF stock. The company gets its money today and effectively sells the stock at the higher price in the future upon conversion.
- To allow companies to access an additional pool of capital. If the company has already issued equity and straight debt, it has tapped the two largest pools of capital. However, there are investors who only buy converts, so the company has to issue a convert to tap into this market.

Income Bonds

An income bond is a bond where the company only pays interest if it can afford to do so. With all of the bonds above income bonds in the capital structure, the company has an absolute obligation to pay interest on time. If they fail, it causes a default and the bond-holders can have the company thrown into bankruptcy to protect their interests. While paying interest on income bonds is optional, management has numerous incentives to make the interest payments in full and on time. If the interest isn't paid there are:

- No management raises or bonuses
- No stock buybacks or dividends
- No acquisitions

CHAPTER TWO

Single Cash Flow Yield Calculations

In the world of investment math, a vehicle offering a 3.97% return can offer a higher return than an investment offering a 4.05% return. This is because yields for different vehicles are quoted assuming different compounding conversions and calendar conventions. The next few chapters discuss investment math. The people who often have the hardest time working with investment math are mathematicians. This is because many of the investment math calculations done on Wall Street are mathematically incorrect.

The place to start any discussion of investment math is with a discussion of present value (PV) / future value (FV) calculations used for investments that only have two cash flows: one out and one in. There are six formulas that are used to perform PV/FV calculations on problems with two cash flows.

SIMPLE INTEREST:

$$FV = PV \times (1 + (R \times T))$$
$$PV = FV / (1 + (R \times T))$$

COMPOUND INTEREST:

$FV = PV \times (1 + R)^n$

$PV = FV / (1 + R)^n$

CONTINUOUS COMPOUNDING:

$FV = PVe^{rt}$

$PV = FV / e^{rt}$

While the formulas are fairly simple, the difficulty is in using the right formula at the right time.

SIMPLE INTEREST

The term simple interest means that all of the interest (I) is paid when the investment matures. Thus, there is no opportunity to reinvest any intermittent interest payments in order to earn interest on interest (IOI). When an investment pays simple interest, the amount of interest that is earned can be calculated via the formula shown in Figure 2.1:

FIGURE 2.1

Calculating Simple Interest

$I = PV \times R \times T$

Where:

I = the amount of interest earned

PV = the amount of principal invested (the present value)

R = the rate at which the principal is invested

T = the amount of time the investment lasts

The total value at the conclusion of the investment (the future value) is equal to the sum of the PV + I. By rearranging this equation, an equation can be derived to solve for the PV that has to be invested today in order to accumulate a certain FV over a given time frame. First, replace the I with the formula for I.

$$FV = PV + I$$
$$FV = PV + (PV \times R \times T)$$

Second, factor out PV on the right side of the equation:

$$FV = PV \times [1 + (1 \times R \times T)]$$

Third, within the parentheses, the 1 can be eliminated since anything multiplied by 1 equals itself, as shown in Figure 2.2.

FIGURE 2.2

Simple Interest Calculation of Future Value

$$FV = PV \times [1 + (R \times T)]$$

Fourth, divide both sides of the equation by the quantity: $[1 + (R \times T)]$ resulting in the equation shown in Figure 2.3.

FIGURE 2.3

Simple Interest Calculation of Present Value

$$PV = FV / [1 + (R \times T)]$$

While the formulas appear to be very simple and straight-forward, they hold a trap for the unwary. The trap in the above equations is the T component. There are at least three alternative conventions for measuring time, and different investment vehicles use different conventions. Before any of the above equations can be solved, it is essential to determine which calendar convention is appropriate for the investment vehicle. Consider the next example, which illustrates the significance of the investment vehicle's calendar convention.

Suppose an investor invests $1MM for 9 months at 10% in a vehicle which pays simple interest. How much interest will the investor earn? The formula for interest is:

$$I = PV \times R \times T$$

The PV ($1MM) and R (10%) components are self-explanatory. The T component, however, can be expressed using a variety of alternative calendar conventions. If the investment vehicle uses an actual/actual (A/A) calendar convention then the "T" component would equal the:

$$\frac{\text{Actual Number of Days in the Investment Period}}{\text{Actual Number of Days in a Year}}$$

If there were 273 days in the 9-month period, the time component would be 273/365 (or 273/366 if the year is a leap year). The amount of interest earned would therefore be:

$$I = \$1MM \times .10 \times 273 / 365$$
$$I = \$74,794.52$$

However, if the investment vehicle uses a 30/360 calendar convention, every month is assumed to have 30 days—regardless of the actual number of days in the month. Thus, in February, the investment pays, and the investor receives, 30 days of interest—even though the month normally has only 28 days. Likewise, in December the investment pays and the investor receives the same 30 days of interest—even though the month has 31 days. Since, in a 30/360 calendar convention, every month has 30 days, a year is assumed to have 360 days. Thus, the time component would be:

$$\frac{\text{Number of Days in the Investment}}{\text{Period Assuming a 30-Day Date Count}}{360}$$

The amount of interest earned would therefore be:

I = $1MM × .10 × 270 / 360
I = $75,000

A third commonly used calendar convention in the United States is Actual/360 (A/360). Under this calendar convention, the time component is equal to:

$$\frac{\text{Actual Number of Days in the Investment Period}}{360}$$

It is obviously inconsistent to use an actual-day count in the numerator while using 360 in the denominator. Yet, this is a very commonly used convention particularly with money market instruments. If the investment uses an A/360 calendar convention, the interest calculation would be:

I = $1MM × .10 × 273 / 360
I = $75,833.33

Thus, depending upon the calendar convention, the amount of interest earned in this example could be $74,794.52, $75,000, or

$75,833.33—a difference that any investor would regard as significant. The calendar conventions for some of the common US investment vehicles are listed in Figure 2.4.

FIGURE 2.4

US Calendar Conventions and Associated Vehicles

Calendar Convention	Applicable Vehicles
A/A	US Treasury bonds
30/360	US corporate bonds Municipal bonds US agencies Eurobonds Mortgages CMOs Fixed side of swaps
A/360	Repurchase agreements Bankers' acceptances Commercial paper Treasury bills Floating side of swaps

While the three calendar conventions in Figure 2.4 are the principal conventions used in the United States, there are a wide variety of other calendar conventions used in other countries, including 365/365, 365/360, and A/365. The only difference between an actual-day count and a 365-day count is that the actual-day count accounts for the extra day in a leap year. Thus, in 3 years out of 4, a 365-day count and an actual-day count are the same. Only if the investment extends into leap year do the two conventions vary. Figure 2.5 lists the calendar conventions of many common non-dollar instruments.

FIGURE 2.5

Calendar Conventions for Common Non-US Instruments

Calendar Convention	Representative Markets
A/365	Japanese government bonds (JGBs) British government bonds (Gilts)
30/360	German government bonds (Bunds) Dutch government bonds (Guilders)
A/A	French government bonds (OATS) Most emerging markets

As you can see, in order to calculate interest, it is often necessary to calculate the number of days between two dates using either an A- or 360-day count. Fortunately, both Excel and the HP-12C calculator include functions that calculate the number of days between two dates using either convention. The procedures to calculate the number of days between two dates are:

IN EXCEL
1. Format two cells as date cells.
2. Put the start date in one cell and the end date in the other.
3. For an actual-day count, in a third cell (formatted as a number) simply subtract the earlier date from the later date.
4. For a 30-day count, in a third cell, insert the "days360" function by typing: =days360(start date, end date)

FOR THE HP-12C
1. Tap the [g] key to activate the blue function keys and then tap the M.DY key (located on the same key as the number 5) to make sure your calculator's default is set to expect dates to be entered in a month-day-year (US) format. This only has to

be done once, unless the default was changed to the day-month-year (European) format by tapping the [g] key followed by the D.MY key located under the eight key. Once the default has been set to the US convention:

2. Type in the start date (defined as the day the investment starts paying interest) using the MM.DDYYYY format.
3. Hit the [ENTER] key so that the calculator knows that the first number is completed.
4. Type the maturity date using the same MM.DDYYYY format.
5. Tap the [g] key and the [ΔDYS] key (located on the same key as the [EEX] key) to calculate the actual number of days between the two dates.
6. To convert the actual-day count to a 360-day count, tap the [X><Y] key.

For example, suppose on January 6, 1995, you invest $1MM in an investment that yields 10% and matures on October 10, 1995. How much interest will you earn assuming the investment uses an A/A, 30/360, and A/360 calendar convention?

STEP 1

Calculate the number of days between the two dates on both an actual- and 30-day count basis:

KEYSTROKES:
   1.061995 [ENTER]
   10.101995 [g] [ΔDYS] = 277 (actual)
   [X><Y]= 274 (360)

STEP 2

Once the number of days has been determined, that number can be used to calculate the amount of interest earned assuming different calendar conventions.

$I = PV \times R \times T$

Using an A/A Calendar: $I = \$1MM \times .1 \times 277 / 365$
  $= \$75,890.41$

Using an A/360 Calendar: $I = \$1MM \times .1 \times 277 / 360$
  $= \$76,944.44$

Using a 30/360 Calendar: $I = \$1MM \times .1 \times 274 / 360$
  $= \$76,111.11$

Before proceeding on to the next section, confirm your understanding of calendar conventions and simple interest by reviewing these next sample problems.

PROBLEM 2A

What is the PV of a $1 return in 6 months assuming an 8% 30/360 simple interest rate?

ANSWER:
  $PV = FV / [1 + (R \times T)]$
  $PV = \$1 / [1 + (.08 \times 180 / 360)]$
  $PV = \$1 / 1.04$
  $PV = .9615384615$

PROBLEM 2B

What is the PV of a $1 return that will be received in 9 months (273 days) assuming a 12% A/360 simple interest?

ANSWER:
  $PV = FV / [1 + (R \times T)]$
  $PV = \$1 / [1 + (.12 \times 273 / 360)]$
  $PV = \$1 / 1.091$
  $PV = .9165902841$

PROBLEM 2C

What is the PV of a $1 return received in 1 year assuming that the dollar is discounted first by 8% simple interest 30/360 for 3 months and then by 9% simple interest 30/360 for 9 months?

ANSWER:

STEP 1

Discount the $1 for the 3-month period:

$PV = FV / [1 + (R \times T)]$

$PV = 1 / [1 + (.08 \times 90 / 360)]$

$PV = 1 / 1.02$

$PV = .9803921569$

STEP 2

Discount the PV in Step 1 for the additional 9 months:

$PV = FV / [1 + (R \times T)]$

$PV = .9803921569 / [1 + (.09 \times 270 / 360)]$

$PV = .9803921569 / 1.0675$

$PV = .9184001469$

PROBLEM 2D

How long will it take to earn at least $100,000 in interest if you invest $1MM in an investment which yields 12% simple interest on an A/A basis?

ANSWER:

$I = PV \times R \times T$

$\$100,000 = \$1MM \times .12 \times A / 365$

$A = (\$100,000 / \$120,000) \times 365$

$A = 304.17 = 305 \text{ days}$

PROBLEM 2E

How long will it take to earn $100,000 in interest if you invest $1MM in an investment which yields 12% simple interest on a 30/360 basis?

ANSWER:

$I = PV \times R \times T$

$\$100,000 = \$1,000,000 \times .12 \times A / 360$

$A = \$100,000 / \$120,000 \times 360$

$A = 300 \text{ days}$

PROBLEM 2F

How much interest will you earn if you invest $1MM on January 12, 1997, until August 27, 1997, at 8% simple interest assuming the yield is expressed on an A/360 basis?

ANSWER:

$I = PV \times R \times T$

$I = \$1,000,000 \times .08 \times 227 / 360$

$I = \$50,444.44$

PROBLEM 2G

How much interest will you earn if you invest $1MM on January 12, 1997, until August 27, 1997, at 8% simple interest assuming the yield is expressed on a 30/360 basis?

ANSWER:

$I = PV \times R \times T$

$I = \$1,000,000 \times .08 \times 225 / 360$

$I = \$50,000.00$

PROBLEM 2H

What rate will allow $1MM to grow to $1.1MM in 1 year assuming simple interest quoted on an A/360 basis?

ANSWER:
$I = PV \times R \times T$
$\$100,000 = \$1,000,000 \times R \times 365 / 360$
$R = 9.86\%$

PROBLEM 2I

You want to earn $50,000 of interest on a $1MM investment over a 9-month period that has 273 days. What rate would you have to earn on a 30/360 calendar?

ANSWER:
$I = PV \times R \times T$
$\$50,000 = \$1MM \times R \times 270 / 360$
$R = \$50,000 / \$1MM \times 360 / 270$
$R = 6.67\%$

PROBLEM 2J

You want to earn $50,000 of interest on a $1MM investment over a 9-month period that has 273 days in it. What rate would you have to earn on an A/360 calendar?

ANSWER:
$I = PV \times R \times T$
$\$50,000 = \$1MM \times R \times 273 / 360$
$R = \$50,000 / \$1MM \times 360 / 273$
$R = 6.59\%$

PROBLEM 2K

You want to earn $50,000 of interest on a $1MM investment over a 9-month period that has 273 days in it. What rate would you have to earn on an A/A calendar?

ANSWER:

$I = PV \times R \times T$

$\$50,000 = \$1MM \times R \times 273 / 365$

$R = \$50,000 / 1MM \times 365 / 273$

$R = 6.68\%$

PROBLEM 2L

How much would you have to invest today in order to earn $500K in interest over 7 months, assuming the 7-month period had 213 days and the investment yields 12%, quoted on an A/360 day basis?

ANSWER:

$I = PV \times R \times T$

$\$500,000 = PV \times .12 \times 213 / 360$

$PV = \$500,000 / (.12 \times 213 / 360)$

$PV = \$7,042,253.52$

PROBLEM 2M

What simple interest rate would you have to earn on an investment quoted on an A/360 calendar in order to earn the same amount of interest you would earn if you invested for 1 year at 10% simple interest quoted on a 30/360 calendar?

ANSWER:

Choose any notional amount—I used $1 in this example.

$PV \times R \times T = PV \times R \times T$

$1 × .1 × 360 / 360 = $1 × R × 365 / 360

.1 = R × 365 / 360

R = (.1 × 360 / 365)

R = 9.86%

PROBLEM 2N

What simple interest rate of return would you have to earn on a 9-month (273 days) investment, quoted on an A/360 calendar, in order to earn the same amount of interest as you would earn on a 7.53% 30/360 investment over the same time period?

ANSWER:

Choose any notional amount—I used $1 in this example.

PV × R × T = PV × R × T

$1 × .0753 × 270 / 360 = $1 × R × 273 / 360

.0753 × 270/360 = R × 273 / 360

.056475 = R × 273 / 360

R = 7.44%

PROBLEM 2O

How much interest accrues *daily* on a $100MM position of 10% Treasuries that mature on April 15, 1998, during the month of February 1987?

ANSWER:

I = PV × R × T

I = $100,000,000 × .05 × 1 / 182

I = $27,472.53

PROBLEM 2P

How much interest accrues *daily* on a $100MM position of 10% Treasuries that mature on April 15, 1998, during the month of July 1986?

ANSWER:
$I = PV \times R \times T$
$I = \$100MM \times .05 \times 1 / 183 = \$27,322.40$

PROBLEM 2Q

Suppose on January 15, 1997, you settle the purchase of $1 billion worth of 10% US Treasuries that mature in 1 year, priced at par. If you reinvest the coupon at 4% 30/360, what is your FV?

ANSWER:
$I = PV \times R \times T$
$I = \$1,000,000,000 \times .1 \times 181 / 365$
$I = \$49,589,041.10$
$I = \$1,000,000,000 \times .1 \times 184 / 365$
$I = \$50,410,958.90$
$IOI = \$49,589,041.10 \times .04 \times 180 / 360$
$IOI = \$991,780.82$
$TOTAL = \$100,991,780.82$

PROBLEM 2R

Suppose on July 15, 1997, you settle the purchase of $1 billion worth of 10% US Treasuries that mature in 1 year priced at par. If you reinvest the coupon at 4% SA 30/360, what is your FV?

ANSWER:

$I = P \times R \times T$

$I = \$1,000,000,000 \times .1 \times 184 / 365$

$I = \$50,410,958.90$

$I = \$1,000,000,000 \times .1 \times 181 / 365$

$I = \$49,589,041.10$

$IOI = \$50,410,958.90 \times .04 \times 180 / 360$

$IOI = \$1,008,219.18$

$TOTAL = \$101,008,219.18$

PROBLEM 2S

What simple interest rate expressed on an A/360 basis would you have to earn in order to quadruple your money assuming you invested on January 1, 1990, and the investment matured on January 1, 2000?

ANSWER:

$FV = PV + (PV \times R \times T)$

$\$4 = \$1 + (\$1 \times R \times 3,652 / 360)$

$\$3 = (\$1 \times R \times 3,652 / 360)$

$\$3 = \$10.144444 \times R$

$R = .295728$

$R = 29.57\%$

PROBLEM 2T

What rate would you have to earn in order to double your money in a year, assuming an A/A, A/360, and 30/360 calendar convention simple interest?

ANSWER:

For A/A:

$I = PV \times R \times T$

$1 = 1 \times R \times 365 / 365$
R=100% A/A

For 30/360:
$I = PV \times R \times T$
$1 = 1 \times R \times 360 / 360$
R=100% 30/360

For A/360:
$1 = 1 \times R \times 365 / 360$
R = 98.63% A/360

CHAPTER THREE

Discount Instruments

Instead of paying interest periodically or at maturity, some instruments do not pay interest at all in the traditional sense. Instead, they are sold at a discount to their face value and return their face value upon maturity. The difference between the instrument's discounted price at purchase and its payment of face value at maturity represents the investor's return.

The return of discounted instruments is quoted on a discounted basis. This means the discount rate is quoted instead of the instrument's effective return. Unfortunately, quoting discounts tends to understate the investment's true return, and this complicates the task of comparing the relative returns of investments that are interest-bearing with discounted instruments. Consider the following example:

A discounted investment with a 1-year maturity is priced at a 10% discount and is quoted on a 30/360 calendar. What would an interest-bearing instrument have to yield in order to offer the same return?

For instruments that are quoted on a discounted basis, the process for calculating the interest-bearing yield equivalent is:

STEP 1

Determine the discount:

Discount = Face Value × Rate × Time

In this example the discount would be:

Discount = $1MM × .10 × 360 / 360 = $100,000
So the purchase price is $1MM − $100,000
= $900,000

STEP 2

Determine the yield:

In this example, the investor earns $100,000 on a
$900,000 investment. This equates to a return of:
$100,000 / $900,000 = 11.11%

Note the return is higher than an interest-bearing investment at
10% 30/360 because in an interest-bearing instrument the investor
earns $100,000 on $1MM. In a discounted instrument, the investor
earns $100,000 on just $900,000.

Let's review some additional calculations before proceeding:

PROBLEM 3A

Convert a 7% 30/360 discount to an interest-bearing equivalent.
Assume an FV of $1 and calculate the discount using the 7% rate.

ANSWER:

Discount = $1 × .07 × 360 / 360
Discount = $.07

Interest equivalent is: $.07 / .93 × 360 / 360 = .0752

= 7.52%

PROBLEM 3B

Convert a 6% A/360 discount yield to an interest-bearing equivalent.

ANSWER:

Discount = $1 × .06 × 365 / 360

Discount = $.0608 = 6.08%

Interest equivalent is: $.0608 / .9392 × 365 / 360 = .0656

= 6.56%

CHAPTER FOUR

Multiple Cash Flows

If the investment pays interest periodically, the FV can be calculated as a series of simple interest problems, as shown in Figure 4.1.

FIGURE 4.1

Calculating FV on Investments That Pay Periodically

Period 1	Period 2	Period 3	Period 4
Jan. 15 2013	July 15 2013	Jan. 15 2014	July 15 2014	Jan. 15 2015
181 Days	184 Days	181 Days	184 Days

FOR PERIOD 1:

$\quad$ PV = \$1,000,000

$\quad$ I = PV × R × T

$\quad$ I = \$1,000,000.00 × .10 × 181 / 365

$\quad$ I = \$49,589.04

FOR PERIOD 2:

PV = $1,000,000 + $49,589.04

I = PV × R × T

I = $1,049,589.04 × .1 × 184 / 365

I = $52,910.79

FOR PERIOD 3:

PV = $1,049,589.04 + $52,910.79

I = PV × R × T

I = $1,102,499.83 × .1 × 181 / 365 = $54,671.91

FOR PERIOD 4:

PV = $1,102,499.83 + $54,671.91

I = PV × R × T

I = $1,157,171.74 × .1 × 184/365

I = $58,334.14

The FV = $1,215,505.88, and the total interest earned is, therefore, $215,505.88.

Calculating Long-Term Returns

While this methodology will always work, it is impractical for long-term problems. Who wants to break a 30-year semiannual bond problem into 60 simple interest problems?

If, *and only if*, the investment vehicle uses a 30/360 calendar convention *and* the investment term is equal to a whole number of compounding periods, then the PV, I, and FV can be calculated using the equation shown in Figure 4.2.

FIGURE 4.2

Calculate FV Using Periodic Compounding

$$FV = PV(1 + i)^n$$

WHERE:

n = number of compounding periods

i = interest rate per compounding period

PV = the number of dollars that are invested

FV = the principal plus the interest at the end of the investment

The equation shown in Figure 4.2 can always be solved using any calculator with an exponent function. (Sometimes it is easier to use the exponent key to solve simple PV/FV problems than it is to use the specialized PV/FV keys.) The HP-12C financial calculator includes a set of keys which are pre-programmed to solve PV/FV equations. The use of these keys is described in Figure 4.3.

FIGURE 4.3

Excel and HP-12C Inputs for PV/FV Calculations

Key	Notes
n	The total # of compounding periods over the life of the investment
i	Interest rate per period (the annual stated interest rate divided by the number of periods per year)
PV	The amount invested (entered as a negative number)
PMT	For zero coupon bond problems—set to zero
FV	Future value of the investment

The following examples illustrate both methodologies of solving simple finite compounding problems.

PROBLEM 4A

You invest $1MM in a 10% 5-year investment which pays interest annually and is quoted on a 30/360 calendar. What is the future value?

ANSWER:

$$FV = PV(1 + i)^n$$
$$FV = \$1MM(1 + .1)^5$$
$$FV = \$1,610,510$$

Keystrokes using exponent key:

1 [ENTER]
.1 +
5 y^x
1,000,000 ×
$1,610,510

Keystrokes using PV/FV keys:

5 [n]
10 [i]
1,000,000 [CHS] [PV]
0 [PMT]
[FV]

PROBLEM 4B

How much would you have to invest today in order to have $5MM in 20 years? Assume you could invest in a vehicle investment that compounds semiannually at 8% on a 30/360 calendar.

ANSWER:

$FV = PV(1 + i)^n$

$\$5MM = PV[1 + .08 / 2]^{40}$

$\$5MM = PV(1 + .04)^{40}$

$\$5MM = 4.08010206 PV$

$PV = \$1,041,445.22$

PROBLEM 4C

What rate would you have to earn in order to turn $1MM into $5MM in 10 years? Assume you can invest in a vehicle that compounds monthly.

ANSWER:

$FV = PV(1 + i)^n$

$\$5MM = \$1MM(1 + i / 12)^{120}$

$5 = (1 + i / 12)^{120}$

$1.013502 = (1 + i / 12)$

$i = .013502$ per period

$i = .013502 \times 12 = .162$

$i = 16.2\%$

PROBLEM 4D

How long will it take for $1MM to become $2MM? Assume that you can invest in a vehicle that yields 10% on a semiannual 30/360 basis.

ANSWER:

$FV = PV(1 + i)^n$

$\$2MM = \$1MM(1 + .05)^n$

$2 = (1 + .05)^n$

$n = 14.21$

Note in this problem the solution from using the exponent keys will be different than the answer from using the PV/FV. This is because using the PV/FV keys on the HP-12C calculates the minimum number of *whole periods* required to achieve the objective. The exponent keys will work with partial periods. Continue to work through the following problems before moving on to the next section.

PROBLEM 4E

How much would you have to invest today in order to have $1MM in 1 year? Assume that you could earn 12% in an investment that compounds monthly and is quoted on a 30/360 basis.

ANSWER:

$PV = FV / [(1 + YTM / PPY)^n]$

$PV = \$1MM / [(1 + .12 / 12)^{12}]$

$PV = \$1MM / [(1 + .01)^{12}]$

$PV = \$887,449.23$

PROBLEM 4F

How much would you have to invest today in order to have $1MM in 1 year? Assume that you could earn 12% in an investment that compounds daily and is quoted on a 30/360 basis.

ANSWER:

$PV = FV / [(1 + YTM / PPY)^n]$

$PV = \$1MM / [(1 + .12 / 360)^{360}]$

$PV = \$1MM / [(1 + .00033333)^{360}]$

$PV = \$886,938.28$

PROBLEM 4G

Assume that you invest $1MM in an investment that yields 10% on a 30/360 calendar and compounds monthly. How long will it take to double your money?

ANSWER:
$FV = PV[(1 + YTM / PPY)^n]$
$\$2MM = \$1MM[(1 + .10 / 12)^n]$
$2 = [(1 + .10 / 12)^n]$
$2 = 1.008333^n$
83.49

PROBLEM 4H

How much interest will you earn if you invest $1MM on January 12, 1997, until August 27, 1997, at 8%? Assume that the yield is expressed on an A/360 basis and that the investment compounds daily.

ANSWER:
$FV = PV[1 + (YTM / PPY)]^n$
$FV = \$1MM[1 + (.08 / 360)]^{227}$
$FV = \$1,051,732.49$
$I = \$51,732.49$

PROBLEM 4I

You invest $1MM in an investment that yields 10% on an A/360 basis and compounds daily. How much will you have at the end of a year?

ANSWER:

$FV = PV[1 + (YTM / PPY)]^n$

$FV = \$1MM[1 + (.10 / 360)]^{365}$

$FV = \$1,106,691.45$

PROBLEM 4J

What is the market value of a \$1MM 30-year euro ZCB that's priced to offer a 12% YTM?

ANSWER:

$PV = FV / [1 + (YTM / PPY)]^n$

$PV = \$1MM / [1 + .12 / 1]^{30}$

$PV = \$33,377.92$

PROBLEM 4K

What is the market value of a \$1MM 30-year US corporate ZCB that's priced to offer a 12% YTM?

ANSWER:

$PV = FV / [1 + (YTM / PPY)]^n$

$PV = \$1MM / [1 + .12 / 2]^{60}$

$PV = \$30,314.34$

PROBLEM 4L

What will \$1MM grow to in 1 year when invested in an instrument with a 10% return and the compounding frequencies listed?

$FV_{AN} = \$1MM (1 + .10)^1$

$FV_{SA} = \$1MM (1 + .10 / 2)^2$

$FV_Q = \$1MM (1 + .10 / 4)^4$

$$FV_M = \$1MM \, (1 + .10 / 12)^{12}$$
$$FV_D = \$1MM \, (1 + .10 / 360)^{360}$$

Compounding Frequency	n	i	PV	PMT	Future Value
Annual (AN)	1	10	-1MM	0	$1,100,000.00
Semiannual (SA)	2	5	-1MM	0	$1,102,500.00
Quarterly (Q)	4	2.5	-1MM	0	$1,103,812.89
Monthly (M)	12	10/12	-1MM	0	$1,104,713.07
Daily (D)	360	10/360	-1MM	0	$1,105,155.57

PROBLEM 4M

What rate will grow $1 to $2 over a 1-year time frame for each of the alternative compounding frequencies listed?

$$SR_{AN} = FV = PV \, (1 + r / 1)^1$$
$$SR_{SA} = FV = PV \, (1 + r / 2)^2$$
$$SR_{Q} = FV = PV \, (1 + r / 4)^4$$
$$SR_{M} = FV = PV \, (1 + r / 12)^{12}$$
$$SR_{D} = FV = PV \, (1 + r / 360)^{360}$$

Compounding Frequency	n	PV	PMT	FV	Periodic i	Effective Return	Stated Return
Annual	1	-1	0	2	100%	100%	100%
Semiannual	2	-1	0	2	41.42%	100%	82.84%
Quarterly	4	-1	0	2	18.92%	100%	75.68%
Monthly	12	-1	0	2	5.95%	100%	71.36%
Daily	360	-1	0	2	.1927%	100%	69.38%

Note that in this problem, in every case, the investment doubles over the course of a year. Effectively, the investor earns a 100% return. The stated returns, however, vary depending upon the compounding frequency. Investments are quoted in the market place based on their *stated return*.

Stated and Effective Returns

Much of the confusion surrounding the real return of investments that compound stems from the way that the returns of investments are quoted. The returns of investments which compound are typically quoted by their *stated returns* instead of the *effective annual return*.

The stated return, as illustrated in Problem 4M, is equal to the interest rate per period simply multiplied by the number of periods per year. It *does not* take the impact of compounding into account. The effective return is the annual rate that the investor actually earns on the original invested capital—including the impact of compounding. Needless to say, this makes comparative analysis of alternative investment vehicles with very different compounding frequencies a bit complicated. Thus, investments should always be compared on the basis of their effective returns, not their stated returns.

Returns Based on Differing Compounding Frequencies

Most investments have predetermined compounding frequencies. For example, eurobonds compound annually; US Treasuries, US corporates, and US municipals compound semiannually; while mortgages and many collateralized mortgage obligations compound monthly. If there is any doubt about the frequency at which an investment compounds, it is best to note it using the notation in Figure 4.4.

FIGURE 4.4

Common Compounding Frequencies

Quote	Interpretation
AN	Annual rate expressed annually
SA	Semiannual rate expressed annually
M	Monthly rate expressed annually
W	Weekly rate expressed annually
D	Daily rate expressed annually

Very often, it is necessary to convert a stated yield based on one calendar conversion to another. To convert a rate expressed on one compounding frequency to its equivalent rate using another compounding frequency, use the formula shown in Figure 4.5. (PPY = payments per year.)

FIGURE 4.5

Rate Conversion

$$\left[1+\frac{r_1}{PPY}\right]^n = \left[1+\frac{r_2}{PPY}\right]^n$$

The following examples illustrate the application of this equation to doing rate conversions.

PROBLEM 4N

What rate would a zero coupon investment that compounds monthly have to earn in order to offer the same effective return as a 10% investment that compounds annually?

$$\left[1+\frac{r_1}{PPY}\right]^n = \left[1+\frac{r_2}{PPY}\right]^n$$

Enter the stated interest rate (.1) and the periods per year (1) of the known investment, and the periods per year for the conversion (12).

$$\left[1+\frac{r_1}{12}\right]^{12} = \left[1+\frac{.1}{1}\right]^{1}$$

$$\left[1+\frac{r_1}{12}\right]^{12} = 1.1$$

After simplifying the right side of the equation, take the 12th root of each side of the equation. Taking the 12th root of a number is the same as raising it to the 1/12th power. Thus to take the 12th root of 1.1, tap the following keystrokes:

Enter:
   1.1 [ENTER]
   12 [1/X] [Y≷X]

$$\left[1+\frac{r_1}{12}\right] = 1.00797414$$

Subtract 1 from both sides of the equation:

$$\left[\frac{r_1}{12}\right] = .00797414$$

Multiply both sides of the equation by 12:
   $r_1 = 9.57\%$

An alternative way of executing a conversion would be use the PV/FV keys. Alternatively, $1 invested for 1 year in a 10% investment which compounds annually will grow to $1.1. Thus, to convert to a monthly rate using the HP-12C would require:

Pay At	End
n	12
i	?
PV	-$1
PMT	0
FV	$1.1
? × 12 =	9.57%

PROBLEM 40

What rate would a zero coupon investment that compounds daily on a 30/360 basis have to earn in order to offer the same effective return as a 10% investment that compounds semiannually?

$$\left[1 + \frac{r_1}{PPY}\right]^n = \left[1 + \frac{r_2}{PPY}\right]^n$$

$$\left[1 + \frac{r_1}{360}\right]^{360} = \left[1 + \frac{.1}{2}\right]^2$$

$$\left[1 + \frac{r_1}{360}\right]^{360} = \left[1 + .05\right]^2$$

$$\left[1 + \frac{r_1}{360}\right]^{360} = 1.1025$$

$$\left[1 + \frac{r_1}{360}\right] = 1.00027109$$

$$r_1 = 9.76\%$$

Alternatively, $1 invested for 1 year in a 10% investment that compounds semiannually will grow to become $1.1025.

Pay At	End
n	2
I	5
PV	-1
PMT	0
FV	?
FV	1.1025

Thus, to convert to a daily rate using the HP-12C would require:

Pay At	End
n	360
I	?
PV	-$1
PMT	0
FV	$1.1025
? × 360 =	9.76%

PROBLEM 4P

What rate would a zero coupon investment that compounds daily on an A/360 basis have to earn in order to offer the same effective return as a 10% investment that compounds annually?

Since this investment compounds daily and is quoted on an A/360 basis the formula for solving for the rate is:

$$\left[1+\frac{r_1}{PPY}\right]^n = \left[1+\frac{r_2}{PPY}\right]^n$$

$$\left[1+\frac{r_1}{360}\right]^{365} = \left[1+\frac{.1}{1}\right]^1$$

$$\left[1+\frac{r_1}{360}\right]^{365} = 1.1$$

$$\left[1+\frac{r_1}{360}\right] = 1.00026116$$

$$r_1 = 9.40\%$$

Alternatively, \$1 invested for 1 year in a 10% investment that compounds annually will grow to \$1.1. Thus, to convert to a daily rate expressed annually using the HP-12C would require:

Pay At	End
n	365
I	?
PV	-\$1
PMT	0
FV	\$1.1
? × 360 =	9.40

Thus, all other factors being equal, the higher the compounding frequency, the higher the effective return. While the previous problems stopped with daily compounding, there is no reason why compounding could not occur every day, every hour, every minute, every second, every nanosecond, and so on. The ultimate limit of this progression is an infinitesimally small compounding period and an infinite number of compounding periods.

Continuous Compounding

Interest rates expressed on a continuously compounded basis have many applications within the world of finance. For example, many option pricing models are based on the concept of continuous rates, and forward rate calculations are much easier when examined on a continuously compounded basis. Financing rates are often quoted on a continuous compounding basis as well.

Continuous rates are dependent upon "base e." Base e has a value of 2.7183. This number can be calculated one of two ways: The first way, as shown in Figure 4.6, is the limit of the infinite series of 1 divided by the factorials:

FIGURE 4.6

Calculating Base e Using the Limit of the Infinite Series of 1 Divided by the Factorials

$$e = 1 + 1/1! + 1/2! + 1/3! + 1/4! + 1/5! + 1/6! + \text{etc.}$$

Alternatively, the value of "e" can be determined by compounding $1 at 100% and assuming an infinite number of compounding periods (Figure 4.7)—which is really the same calculation in another form.

FIGURE 4.7

Calculating Base e by Compounding $1 at 100% and Assuming an Infinite Number of Compounding Periods

$$\underset{X \to \infty}{e} = \left[1 + \frac{1}{\infty}\right]^{\infty}$$

When the interest rate is compounded continuously, use the formula shown in Figure 4.8 to perform PV/FV calculations.

FIGURE 4.8

PV/FV Calculations for Continuously Compounded Interest

$$FV = PVe^{rt}$$
$$PV = FV/e^{rt}$$

To solve for either the PV or the FV, first multiply the interest rate by the time component. (Remember to use the appropriate calendar convention.) Raise base e to the result by using a hand-held calculator with an e^x key or using the =EXP() function in Excel. Then, solve for either FV (given the PV) or the PV (given the FV).

PROBLEM 4Q

You invest \$1MM for 1 year at 10% continuously compounded (Cc) on a 30/360 calendar basis. What is the future value?

$$FV = PVe^{rt}$$
$$FV = \$1MMe^{(.1 \times 360 / 360)}$$
$$FV = \$1MM(1.1051709181)$$
$$FV = \$1,105,170.92$$

PROBLEM 4R

You invest \$10MM on January 15, 1997, for 6 months at 15% Cc on an A/360 basis. What is your future value?

$$FV = PVe^{rt}$$
$$FV = \$10MMe^{(.15 \times 181 / 360)}$$
$$FV = \$10MM(1.078333629)$$
$$FV = \$10,783,336.29$$

PROBLEM 4S

How much would you have to invest today in order to have $1MM in 9 months? Assume that today is February 15, 1997, and you could earn 12% Cc A/A.

$$FV = PVe^{rt}$$
$$\$1MM = PVe^{(.12 \times 273 / 365)}$$
$$\$1MM = PV(1.0939045206)$$
$$PV = \$914,156.57$$

To solve for either the interest rate or the time component it is necessary to take the inverse of base e which requires taking the natural log (ln)—again using a simple calculator. Taking the natural log of base e raised to a power eliminates the e and brings the entire exponent down to the main line, as shown in Figure 4.9.

FIGURE 4.9

Taking the Natural Log of Base e Raised to a Power

$$\ln(e^x) = X$$

PROBLEM 4T

What rate expressed on a Cc 30/360 basis would allow $1MM to grow to $2MM over a 1-year time frame?

$$FV = PVe^{rt}$$
$$\$2MM = \$1MMe^{(r \times 360 / 360)}$$
$$2 = e^r$$
$$\ln(2) = \ln(e^r)$$
$$.6931 = r$$
$$r = 69.31\%$$

PROBLEM 4U

How long will it take for \$1MM to grow to \$3MM? Assume you have invested at 27.67% Cc 30/360 basis.

$$FV = PVe^{rt}$$
$$\$3MM = \$1MMe^{(.2767t)}$$
$$3 = e^{.2767t}$$
$$\ln(3) = \ln(e^{.2767t})$$
$$1.0986122887 = .2767t$$
$$t = 3.97 \text{ years}$$

PROBLEM 4V

What rate, expressed on an A/360 basis, is required to grow \$1MM to \$2MM? Assume that the money is invested from January 1, 1997, to January 1, 2000.

$$FV = PVe^{rt}$$
$$\$2MM = \$1MMe^{(r \times 1095 / 360)}$$
$$2 = e^{(r \times 1095 / 360)}$$
$$\ln(2) = \ln(e^{(r \times 1095 / 360)})$$
$$.6931 = r \times 1095 / 360$$
$$r = 22.79\%$$

CHAPTER FIVE

Basic Bond Yield Calculations

Bonds have numerous yield measures. Calculating the various yields is not difficult, but using the right yield measure at the right time is often confusing. In this chapter, we'll look at the basic yield measures and the correct circumstance in which to use them.

COUPON YIELD

The coupon yield equals the number of dollars of interest per year divided by the bond's face value. If the bond pays $70 per year, then the coupon is $70/$1,000 = 7%. A coupon yield is only used to describe a bond such as the IBM 7% of June 15, 2043.

Aside from identifying the bond, the current yield has no useful application. The calculation doesn't accurately measure the client's real return because the calculation doesn't include any provision for:

- Buying the bond at a price other than par
- Amortizing any premium or discount

- Assessing the impact of any embedded options
- Reinvesting the interest payments at different rates
- Assessing the impact of taxes
- Assessing the impact of inflation

CURRENT YIELD

The current yield equals the number of dollars in interest per year divided by the current value of the bond. It is sometimes referred to as the cash-on-cash return.

If the 7% IBM bond mentioned in the "Coupon Yield" section was priced at $800, the current return would be 70/800 = 8.75%. If that same 7% bond was priced at $1,150, the current return would be 70/1150 = 6.09%.

This yield calculation makes a provision for the investor buying the bond at a discount or premium—but excludes any provision for:

- Amortizing any premium or discount
- Assessing the impact of any embedded options
- Reinvesting the interest payments at different rates
- Assessing the impact of taxes
- Assessing the impact of inflation

The only investors who are concerned with current return are retirees. Consider the following: A welder retires after 30 years of service. He receives a check for $400,000 and goes to a local brokerage office. He wants the highest yield he can get while only taking a reasonable amount of risk.

Family history suggests a projected longevity of 75 years. His broker builds a portfolio of A rated bonds that have a long maturity

(25–30 years) because they offer the highest yield. Typically, the broker would choose bonds that pay interest in each month, so the retiree would get a monthly interest check. Since the bonds will mature long after the welder is dead, the amortization toward par is of little significance to the welder. The retiree simply wants to know what his or her income will be without touching the principal.

YIELD TO MATURITY

The yield to maturity is the internal rate of return of a bond's cash flows including any accretion or amortization toward par. It is the one yield that, when used to discount the future cash flows, results in the sum of those cash flows equaling the price or PV of the bond.

In other words, the YTM incorporates the bond's interest payments as well as any accretion or amortization to par at maturity, as shown in Figure 5.1.

FIGURE 5.1

YTM Calculation of PV

$$PV = \frac{CF_1}{(1+y)^1} + \frac{CF_2}{(1+y)^2} + \frac{CF_3}{(1+y)^3} \cdots \frac{CF_{Last}}{(1+y)^{Last}}$$

$$PV = \sum_{1}^{n} \frac{CFn}{(1+y)^n}$$

To illustrate, let's look at a 5-year 7% eurobond, which is selling in the secondary market for $910. An investor buying this bond and holding it to maturity would receive $70 per year in interest and $90 in capital accretion spread over 5 years. Entering the data on this bond into the formula depicted in Figure 5.1 would result in the equation shown in Figure 5.2.

FIGURE 5.2

YTM Calculation of a 5-Year 7% Eurobond

$$\$910 = \frac{\$70}{(1+y)^1} + \frac{\$70}{(1+y)^2} + \frac{\$70}{(1+y)^3} + \frac{\$70}{(1+y)^4} + \frac{\$1{,}070}{(1+y)^5}$$

Solving this equation for y (where y represents the yield used to discount the future cash flows) requires an iterative process, which means we try a number, see if the result is too big or too small, and then try another number until we get it right. Suppose we start with 12%, as shown in Figure 5.3.

FIGURE 5.3

12% Yield Used to Discount the Future Cash Flows

$$\frac{\$70}{(1+.12)^1} + \frac{\$70}{(1+.12)^2} + \frac{\$70}{(1+.12)^3} + \frac{\$70}{(1+.12)^4} + \frac{\$1{,}070}{(1+.12)^5}$$

$$\$62.50 + \$55.80 + \$49.82 + \$44.49 + \$607.15$$

$$\$819.76 < \$910, \text{ so } 12\% \text{ is too high.}$$

With the knowledge that 12% is too high, we try 8%, as shown in Figure 5.4.

FIGURE 5.4

8% Yield Used to Discount the Future Cash Flows

$$\frac{\$70}{(1+.08)^1} + \frac{\$70}{(1+.08)^2} + \frac{\$70}{(1+.08)^3} + \frac{\$70}{(1+.08)^4} + \frac{\$1,070}{(1+.08)^5}$$

$$\$64.81 + \$60.01 + \$55.57 + \$51.45 + \$728.22$$

$$\$960.07 < \$910, \text{ so } 8\% \text{ is too low.}$$

With 8% too low and 12% too high, we try 10%, 9%, 9.5%, 9.25%, etc., until we arrive at 9.33%, as shown in Figure 5.5.

FIGURE 5.5

9.33% Yield Used to Discount the Future Cash Flows

$$\frac{\$70}{(1+.0933)^1} + \frac{\$70}{(1+.0933)^2} + \frac{\$70}{(1+.0933)^3} + \frac{\$70}{(1+.0933)^4} + \frac{\$1,070}{(1+.0933)^5}$$

$$\$64.02 + \$58.56 + \$53.56 + \$48.99 + \$684.87$$

$$\$910.07 < \$910, \text{ so } 9.33\% \text{ is the right yield.}$$

The YTM is the most commonly quoted return. It's the return that's quoted in the *Wall Street Journal* and on the brokers' pricing screens. It's the yield that's discussed by the analysts on all the TV shows. However, buying bonds with the highest YTM for a given rating and maturity is rarely the best strategy for investors. This is because YTM makes no provision for:

- Assessing the impact of any embedded options
- Reinvesting the interest payments at different rates

- Assessing the impact of taxes
- Assessing the impact of inflation

Therefore, just because a bond has a YTM of 8.925% does not mean the investor's wealth will increase by 8.925%. Consider the following two bonds:

- ABC—A rated non-call 2% 25-year bond priced at $577.18 to offer a 5% YTM
- DEF—A rated non-call 10% 25-year bond priced at $1,726.50 to offer a 4.9% YTM

Both bonds have the same maturity and credit rating, but ABC offers an extra 10 basis points of YTM. However, this isn't the whole story. Suppose you thought interest rates were going to rise! Which bond would you prefer?

ABC generates only $20 per bond to reinvest at the higher rates as rates rise. On the other hand, DEF generates $100 per bond to reinvest at the higher rate! In order to make a fair comparison, an equal amount of money has to be invested in both bonds. Assuming you do reinvest at 10%, three ABC bonds would grow to be $8,900.82, while one DEF bond would grow to $10,834.71. *The higher coupon is more valuable over time than the extra 10 basis points of YTM.*

In general, if rates are expected to rise, investors should buy bonds with high coupons. Using this strategy, they can quickly reinvest at the higher rates and drag the average return of their portfolios up. If they expect rates to decline, they should buy zero coupon bonds so they don't have to reinvest interest payments at progressively lower rates. From 1982 to 2012, interest rates in the United States declined. Investors who bought 30-year zeros in 1982 enjoyed 30 years of not having to reinvest at progressively lower rates.

Consider the return difference between a 16% 30-year eurobond and a 30-year euro ZCB priced to offer a 16% return over a 30-year period in which rates decline by .5% a year. (Assume a tax-free account.) The ZCB, with no interest payments to reinvest at the lower rates, returns 16%. It costs $11.65 and returns $1,000 in 30 years. Figure 5.6 shows the coupon bond return.

FIGURE 5.6

The 16% Coupon Bond Return

Time	Payment	Reinvestment Rate	Payments + Interest Earned on Interest Paid
0	-$1,000		
1	$160	15%	$184
2	$160	14.5%	$393.88
3	$160	14%	$631.42
4	$160	13.5%	$898.27
5	$160	13%	$1,195.84
6	$160	12.5%	$1,525.32
7	$160	12%	$1,887.56
8	$160	11.5%	$2,283.03
9	$160	11%	$2,711.76
10	$160	10.5%	$3,173.30
11	$160	10%	$3,666.62
12	$160	9.5%	$4,190.15
13	$160	9%	$4,741.67
14	$160	8.5%	$5,318.31
15	$160	8%	$5,916.57
16	$160	7.5%	$6,532.32
17	$160	7%	$7,160.78

Time	Payment	Reinvestment Rate	Payments + Interest Earned on Interest Paid
18	$160	6.5%	$7,796.63
19	$160	6%	$8,434.03
20	$160	5.5%	$9,066.70
21	$160	5%	$9,688.03
22	$160	4.5%	$10,291.20
23	$160	4%	$10,869.24
24	$160	3.5%	$11,415.27
25	$160	3%	$11,922.53
26	$160	2.5%	$12,384.59
27	$160	2%	$12,795.48
28	$160	1.5%	$13,149.81
29	$160	1%	$13,442.91
30	$160	0%	$14,602.91
		Overall Rate	9.349%

The ZCB outperformed the coupon bond by 6.651% before the extra transaction costs of reinvesting were imposed.

In addition, suppose you did some research and discovered that while both bonds have the same "A" credit rating today, last year ABC was rated AA, while DEF was rated BBB. In other words, the credit quality of ABC is declining while the credit quality of DEF is increasing. If these trends continue, then in a few years ABC could be rated BB, while DEF could be rated AA.

Very often the bonds that offer the highest YTMs have the wrong coupon for the market environment (low in a rising rate environment and high in a declining rate environment) and a negative credit trajectory. Be very cautious when selecting bonds based on their YTMs.

Embedded Options

The yield-to-call calculation is identical to the YTM calculation—with the exception that the call price and call date are substituted for the maturity value and maturity date.

The yield-to-put calculation is also is identical to the YTM calculation—with the exception that the put price and put date are substituted for the maturity value and maturity date.

The yield-to-maturity of a sinking fund bond is the weighted average of the various YTMs on the bond's various retirement dates.

The yield-to-worst is the lowest of all the yields.

The flaw in the YTM calculation (and all its associated calculations) is that it looks at the return at a moment in time. Investors have to look at the return over an investment horizon if they are to be successful. Over an investment horizon, the following factors are all quite relevant:

- Rate(s) at which payments are reinvested
- Taxes, and changes in tax rates
- Inflation, and changes in inflation rate

Let's look at some yield measures that incorporate the above variables.

REALIZED COMPOUND YIELD (RCY)

In the YTM calculation, one of two assumptions is made. Either the interest payments:

- Are spent as soon as they are received, so there is no reinvestment issue.

- Are assumed to be reinvested at the same YTM as the bond offered on the day it was bought.

For example, if an investor bought a 20-year 8% bond at par, the YTM calculation assumes that the:

- First interest payment in 6 months will be reinvested for 19.5 years at 8%
- Mid-term interest payment in 10 years will be reinvested for 10 years at 8%
- Last payment before maturity in 19.5 years will be reinvested for 6 months at 8%

For the reinvestment YTM assumption to be true, the yield curve would have to be both fixed and flat. The yield curve is neither flat nor fixed; therefore, this is a stupid assumption.

Instead of assuming that the interest payments are reinvested at the YTM, the RCY calculation assumes different reinvestment rate(s). If, when interest payments come in, they are reinvested in a money market fund, the assumed reinvestment rate should be the money market fund rate. If the investor expects hyperinflation with rates hitting 20%, then 20% should be used for projections. Some investors assume each cash flow will be reinvested at the implied forward rate.

To calculate the RCY, assuming one reinvestment rate, first calculate the T$R which equals P + I + IOI. For this example, since the bond is held to maturity, the P is $1,000. I + IOI can be calculated as a simple PV / FV problem. Looking at a 25-year 7% eurobond priced at par, and assuming a 3% reinvestment rate, the T$R is calculated using the data shown in Figure 5.7.

FIGURE 5.7

In the First Part of RCY Calculation, Calculate the Total "Interest" Plus "Interest on Interest" Earned Over the Entire Investment Time Frame by Using the FV Key

Variable	Definition	Example
n	Number of periods	25
I	Reinvestment rate (per Period)	3%
PV	$0—there is no I or IOI at the start	$0
PMT	Periodic payment	$70
FV	What we are solving for	? = $2,552.15

In other words, 25 payments of $70 compounded at 3% is equal to $2,552.15. Since the interest is $1,750 (25 × $70), the IOI must be $802.15 ($2,552.15 − $1,750). Thus the T$R will be:

$$T\$R = P + I + IOI$$
$$T\$R = \$1,000 + \$1,750 + \$802.15$$
$$T\$R = \$3,225.15$$

Now that we know the T$R, we can calculate the RCY as a second PV / FV problem, using the data shown in Figure 5.8.

FIGURE 5.8

In the 2nd Part of RCY Calculation, the Bond Is Reduced to a Zero Coupon Bond and the Overall Return Is Determined

Variable	Definition	Example
n	Number of periods	25
I	What we are solving for	? = 4.80%
PV	$1,000—price of bond	-$1,000

Variable	Definition	Example
PMT	$0 All payment are in the FV	$0
FV	The T$R	$3,225.15

This passes the reasonable test. With the original principal earning 7% and the reinvestment earning 3%, the overall return has to be somewhere in between the two returns. In this example, only one reinvestment rate was assumed. Of course, a different rate can be assumed for each reinvestment period.

While the RCY calculation accounts for a hopefully realistic assumption about reinvestment risk, it still makes no provision for taxes or inflation. What type of investor has to reinvest but is exempt from taxes *and* inflation? Qualified retirement accounts are exempt from current taxation. However, in order to be exempt from inflation, the liabilities have to be fixed. Certain defined benefit plans have fixed liabilities. For example, suppose a defined benefit plan promises to pay an employee $1MM after 25 years of employment. In this case, the company has to accumulate the $1MM over the 25 years of the employee's employment. If the investment performance is good, the employer's costs are low; if the performance is poor, the costs are higher. The employer assumes the investment risk.

However, since the liability is fixed the employer isn't worried about inflation. The employer's obligation ends with the payment of $1MM. That sum may allow the employer to enjoy a rich and long retirement or may be enough for a single meal, but that is the employee's problem. Depending upon the assumed reinvestment rate, the choice of which bond to buy may be the one with the highest YTM. Consider the two bonds depicted in Figure 5.9.

FIGURE 5.9

High YTM Doesn't Equal Higher RCY

	YTM	RCY
A	7%	4.5%
B	7.2%	4.3%

Since the RCYs are lower than the YTMs, we can conclude that the assumed reinvestment rate is lower than the YTM. Bond B offers a higher YTM, but a lower RCY. The reason Bond B offers a lower RCY is that it has a higher coupon and, therefore, more of its cash flow money is reinvested at the lower rate. Again, if rates are expected to fall, you want to select low coupon bonds; if rates rise, you want to select high coupon bonds.

NET REALIZED COMPOUND YIELD

The RCY calculation can also be performed on an after-tax basis. The after-tax RCY is referred to as the net realized compound yield (NRCY). The investment's after-tax return could be calculated as the overall return from the amount invested to the total number of after-tax dollars accumulated at the end of the investment horizon—the so-called after-tax total dollar return (TR_T).

Tax-Free vs. Taxable Investments

Most investors underestimate the impact of taxes. For example, suppose an investor in the 50% tax bracket buys a 10% eurobond at par. The traditional way in which the after-tax yield of investments is calculated *is only valid when the assumption is made that the interest payments are not reinvested.* Here is the traditional formula:

$$\text{Pre-Tax Yield} \times (1 - \text{Tax Rate}) = \text{After-Tax Return}$$

What is the after-tax return if you reinvest? It is not 5%. It is less than 5%. The reason is depicted in Figure 5.10.

FIGURE 5.10

After-Tax Return Comparison for a Tax-Free Investor and a 50% Tax Rate Investor

		Tax-Free Investor		
Today		1 year		2 year
Start with $1,000	Invest	Receive $100 of I	Reinvest	Receive $10 of IOI
				Receive $100 of I

		50% Tax Rate Investor		
Today		1 year		2 year
Start with $1,000	Invest	Receive $100 of I	Reinvest	Receive $5 of IOI
		Net $50 of I		Net $2.50 IOI
				Receive $100 of I
				Net $50 of I

After 2 years:

- A tax-free investor has $210 ($200 of I and $10 of IOI)
- A taxable investor has $102.50 ($100 of I and $2.50 of IOI)

While a 50% tax rate reduces the interest component by 50%, it reduces the interest-on-interest by 75%. It causes a 75% reduction because the I is dropped by 50%. This reduces the amount reinvested by 50%, which reduces the IOI by 50%. Then, the lower IOI is itself subject to a 50% tax. If I is reduced by 50% and IOI is reduced by 75%, the overall impact of a 50% tax rate is greater than 50%.

Calculating NRCY

Figures 5.11 and 5.12 show examples of NRCY calculation data.

FIGURE 5.11

Calculating the I + IOI on an After-Tax Basis

Variable	Definition	Example
n	Number of periods	25
I	After-tax reinvestment rate	1.5%
PV	$0—there is no I or IOI at the start	$0
PMT	After-tax periodic payment	$35
FV	What we are solving for	$1,052.21

Thus, $T\$R_T$ is $P_T + I_T + IOI_T = \$1,000 + \$875 + \$177.21$
$= \$2,052.21$

FIGURE 5.12

Calculating the Overall Rate

Variable	Definition	Example
n	Number of periods	25
I	What we are solving for	2.92%
PV	$1,000—price of bond	-$1,000
PMT	$0 All payment are in the FV	$0
FV	The T$R	$2,052.21

The NRCY is appropriate for certain types of investors, such as some life insurance companies. Life insurance companies have to reinvest and pay taxes, but because of the laws of statistics, the company's liabilities are effectively fixed. The company may not know which of its policy holders will die, but it knows how many will die and what it will have to pay out. That effectively fixes the company's liabilities and shields it from the impact of inflation.

Consider these two bonds:

- Bond A—8% 20-year eurobond priced at par
- Bond B—2% 20-year eurobond priced to offer a 7.9% YTM

If we assume that the reinvestment rate is 6%, the income tax rate is 40%, and the capital gains rate is 20%, let's compare the NRCYs.

Bond A

After-Tax I + IOI		
n		20
I	After-tax rate (6% × .6)	3.6%
PV		0
PMT	After-tax payment ($80 × .6)	$48
FV	I + IOI After Tax	? = $1,371.46

NRCY		
n		20
I		? = 4.412%
PV	Price	-$1,000
PMT		0
FV	T$R ($1,000 + I + IOI)	$2,371.46

Bond B

After-Tax I + IOI		
n		20
i	After-tax rate (2% × .6)	1.2%
PV		0
PMT	After-tax payment ($20 × .6)	$12
FV	After-tax I + IOI	$269.43

NRCY		
N		20
I		5.22%
PV	Price of bond @ 7.9% YTM	-416.39
PMT		0
FV	$I_T + IOI_T + P_T$ $269.43 + [$1,000 − (($1,000 − $416.39) × .2)]	$1,152.71

Even though Bond B has a lower YTM, it has a higher NRCY because it has a lower coupon and is selling at a discount. A significant part of Bond B's return is taxed at the lower capital gains rate (20%) vs. the higher income tax rate (40%).

NET-NET REALIZED COMPOUND YIELD

The net-net realized compound yield (NNRCY) incorporates different reinvestment rates, taxes, *and* the impact of inflation. If the investor is subject to inflation, the NRCY must also be reduced by the inflation rate. If the NRCY and the inflation rate are expressed using the same compounding frequency and calendar convention, the inflation rate can simply be subtracted from the yield in order to determine the after-inflation yield. For example, if the inflation rate was 3% An/An 30/360, the NNRCY would be calculated as follows:

2.92% − 3% = −.08% or −8 basis points

If the bond's yield and the inflation are not expressed using the same calendar convention and compounding frequency, one rate or the other has to be converted before the inflation rate is subtracted.

For example, if the inflation rate was quoted Q 30/360, the NNRCY would be calculated like this:

$(1 + .03/4)^4 = 3.03\%$
2.92% − 3.03% = −.11% or −11 basis points

Note that depending upon the investor's assumptions regarding the reinvestment rate, the tax rate, and inflation rate, the NNRCY can often be negative. When this happens, don't buy bonds. It is ridiculous to buy bonds when their projected after-tax real return is negative. Instead buy equities, real estate, antiques—anything but bonds.

CHAPTER SIX

Bootstrapping the Zero Coupon Curve

The value of a bond is equal to the PV of each of its future cash flows discounted by the bond's YTM *or* the value of a bond is equal to the present value of each cash flow discounted by its individual spot rate (that is, the yield the cash flow would yield if it was sold as a single cash flow). Figure 6.1 depicts the formula for valuing a bond at a given spot rate.

FIGURE 6.1

Formula for Valuing a Bond Given Spot Rates

$$PV = \frac{CF_1}{(1+SR_1)^1} + \frac{CF_2}{(1+SR_2)^2} + \frac{CF_3}{(1+SR_3)^3} \cdots \frac{CF_{Last}}{(1+SR_L)^{Last}}$$

The "spot rates" can be derived from the cash market rates of new bonds issued at par. Consider the following data for newly issued AAA rated eurobonds:

	Coupon	Price	YTM	Spot Rate
1	7%	$1,000	7%	?
2	8%	$1,000	8%	?
3	9%	$1,000	9%	?
4	10%	$1,000	10%	?

The 1-year bond is a ZCB because it only has one cash flow. The investor buys it for $1,000 and receives $1,070 in 1 year. Thus, the 1-year spot rate and YTM are the same: 7%.

	Coupon	Price	YTM	Spot Rate
1	7%	$1,000	7%	7%
2	8%	$1,000	8%	?
3	9%	$1,000	9%	?
4	10%	$1,000	10%	?

The 2-year bond has two cash flows: $80 in year 1 and $1,080 in year 2. Together, they are offered at an average discount of 8%. However, if they are sold separately, the first cash flow should be sold at a 7% discount because it occurs in 1 year. We can then solve for the second spot rate using the following formula:

$$PV = \frac{\$80}{(1+.07)^1} + \frac{\$1,080}{(1+SR_2)^2}$$

Solving for spot rate 2, we find the second spot rate is 8.04%.

	Coupon	Price	YTM	Spot Rate
1	7%	$1,000	7%	7%
2	8%	$1,000	8%	8.04%
3	9%	$1,000	9%	?
4	10%	$1,000	10%	?

The 3-year bond has three cash flows: $90 in year 1, $90 in year 2, and $1,090 in year 3. Together, they are offered at an average discount of 9%. However, if they are sold separately, the first cash flow should be sold at a 7% discount because it occurs in 1 year, and the second cash flow should be sold at an 8.04% discount. We can then solve for the third spot rate using the following formula:

$$PV = \frac{\$90}{(1+.07)^1} + \frac{\$90}{(1+.0804)^2} + \frac{\$1,090}{(1+SR_3)^3}$$

Solving for spot rate 3, we find the third spot rate is 9.17%.

	Coupon	Price	YTM	Spot Rate
1	7%	$1,000	7%	7%
2	8%	$1,000	8%	8.04%
3	9%	$1,000	9%	9.17%
4	10%	$1,000	10%	?

Continuing with the progression, the 4-year bond has four cash flows: $100 in year 1, $100 in year 2, $100 in year 3, and $1,100 in year 4. Together they are offered at an average discount of 10%. However, if they are sold separately, the first cash flow should be sold at a 7% discount because it occurs in 1 year, the second cash flow should be sold at a discount of 8.04%, the third cash flow should be sold at a discount of 9.17%. We can then solve for the 4th spot rate using the following formula:

$$PV = \frac{\$100}{(1+.07)^1} + \frac{\$100}{(1+.0804)^2} + \frac{\$100}{(1+.0917)^3} + \frac{\$1,100}{(1+SR_4)^4}$$

Solving for spot rate 4, we find it is 10.25%.

	Coupon	Price	YTM	Spot Rate
1	7%	$1,000	7%	7%
2	8%	$1,000	8%	8.04%
3	9%	$1,000	9%	9.17%
4	10%	$1,000	10%	10.25%

Having solved for the spot rates, we can price 4-year AAA rated bonds. Specifically, let's price 3 different 4-year AAA rated bonds—with 0%, 10%, and 20% coupons. Note that as the coupon gets higher, more cash proportionally is discounted at the lower rates. *Thus, bonds with the same credit rating and same maturity will offer different YTMs if they have different coupons.* (See Figure 6.2.)

FIGURE 6.2

Three Different 4-Year Eurobonds with Three Different Coupons

$$PV = \frac{\$0}{(1+.07)^1} + \frac{\$0}{(1+.0804)^2} + \frac{\$0}{(1+.0917)^3} + \frac{\$1,000}{(1+.1025)^4} = \$676.84 = 10.25\%$$

$$PV = \frac{\$100}{(1+.07)^1} + \frac{\$100}{(1+.0804)^2} + \frac{\$100}{(1+.0917)^3} + \frac{\$1,100}{(1+.1025)^4} = \$1,000.00 = 10\%$$

$$PV = \frac{\$200}{(1+.07)^1} + \frac{\$200}{(1+.0804)^2} + \frac{\$200}{(1+.0917)^3} + \frac{\$1,200}{(1+.1025)^4} = \$1,324.18 = 9.81\%$$

The distribution of the bond's cash flows along the yield curve is the key to its valuation.

CHAPTER SEVEN

Valuing Bonds Using the Zero Curve

The value of any investment is the PV of the future cash flows. Consider the following example where you buy a bond in the secondary market that will generate the following five cash flows spaced 1 year apart.

Years				
1	2	3	4	5
$80	$80	$80	$80	$1,080

Since the five cash flows occur at different times, they should be discounted at different rates, as shown in Figure 7.1. In fact, the best way to conceptualize a bond is just that: It is a collection of zero coupon bonds.

FIGURE 7.1

Valuing Bond Using Spot Rates

Bond Cash Flow #	Future Face Value	Appropriate ZCB Rates	Present Value
1	$80	3%	$77.67
2	$80	4%	$73.96
3	$80	4.75%	$69.60
4	$80	5.25%	$65.19
5	$1,080	5.50%	$826.35
		Total	$1,112.78

Each cash flow should be discounted at the appropriate discount rate for when the cash flow occurs. The discount rate would equal the current yield of zero coupon bonds with the same maturity and credit quality. After all, it doesn't make any difference if an AA rated cash flow that comes due in 5 years is sold:

- By itself, as in the case of a zero coupon bond
- As part of a collection of cash flows, as depicted in Figure 7.1

Its present value should be the same.

The present values of the five cash flows were shown in the last column of Figure 7.1. Put simply, the value of the bond is equal to the sum of the present value of the cash flows the investor receives. In this example, the PV equals $1,112.78.

$$PV = \frac{CF1}{(1+SR_1)^1} + \frac{CF2}{(1+SR_2)^2} + \frac{CF3}{(1+SR_3)^3} + \frac{CF4}{(1+SR_4)^4} + \frac{CF5}{(1+SR_5)^5}$$

$$\$1{,}112.78 = \frac{\$80}{(1+.03)^1} + \frac{\$80}{(1+.04)^2} + \frac{\$80}{(1+.0475)^3} + \frac{\$80}{(1+.05)^4} + \frac{\$1{,}080}{(1+.0575)^5}$$

Now, while each cash flow is discounted at a different rate, we need a way to express the overall return. The overall return (YTM) is the weighted average of the individual spot rates.

$$PV = \frac{CF_1}{(1+YTM)^1} + \frac{CF_2}{(1+YTM)^2} + \frac{CF_3}{(1+YTM)^3} + \frac{CF_4}{(1+YTM)^4} + \frac{CF_5}{(1+YTM)^5}$$

Variable	Input
n	5
I	?
PV	-$1,112.78
PMT	80
FV	1,000
Answer	5.37%

Since the yield of the individual cash flows ranges from 3% to 5.5%, the weighted average has to be between those two values. Since the last cash flow at 5.5% is so much larger than the others, it should slant the average toward the high end of 5.5%. Thus, the yield to maturity is 5.37%. While the YTM is 5.37%, it is important that no single cash flow in the bond is offering a return of 5.37%; that is simply the weighted average of the individual spot rates.

Thus, the key to valuing any risk-free bond is to start with the AAA spot curve to find the right discount rates for the future cash flows. Interpolation can be used to fill in any blank spaces in the zero curve. For example, consider the spot yields depicted in Figure 7.2.

FIGURE 7.2

Current Spot Rates

ZCB Maturity	AAA Yields
1	2.20%
3	3.41%
6	4.17%
12	4.93%
24	5.70%
36	6.14%
60	6.80%
120	7.47%
240	8.19%
360	8.67%

Enter the data from Figure 7.2 into Excel, and select "insert chart," "scatter," and then select the chart that plots only the data points. A graph like the one shown in Figure 7.3 should appear.

FIGURE 7.3

X:Y Chart of Data Points

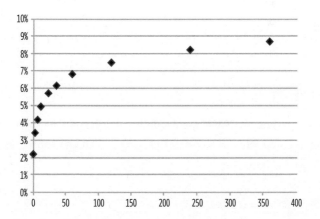

Once the data points are charted, right-click on one data point and select "add trendline." Select the logarithmic alternative, and then check "display equation on chart" and "display R-squared value on chart." Your result should look like Figure 7.4 and display the formula for the yield curve.

FIGURE 7.4

Formula for Yield Curve

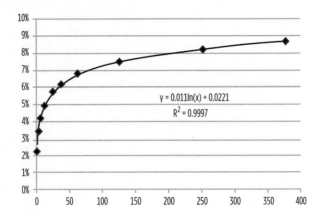

Given this spot curve, solve the following problems.

PROBLEM 7A

What is the price and YTM of a 9-year zero coupon bond?

ANSWER:

Since the bond is a ZCB, there is only one cash flow. The appropriate discount rate can be determined using the regression formula shown in Figure 7.4:

$$y = 0.011\ln(x) + 0.0221$$

Since the bond is a 9-year bond and 9 years is 108 months, the discount rate is:

7.36% monthly rate expressed annually = 0.011 × ln(108)
+ 0.0221)

Discounting $1,000 at a rate of 7.36% / 12 for 108 months
yields = $516.66

PROBLEM 7B

What is the price and YTM of a 10-year 12% eurobond?

ANSWER:

Treat the 10 annual cash flows as individual cash flows and calculate the appropriate discount rates and present values. Then, sum the present values to obtain the price. Use that price to solve for the average yield, the YTM.

Months	Cash Flow	Yield	Price
12	$120	4.94%	$114.35
24	$120	5.71%	$107.39
36	$120	6.15%	$100.32
48	$120	6.47%	$93.39
60	$120	6.71%	$86.71
72	$120	6.91%	$80.35
84	$120	7.08%	$74.32
96	$120	7.23%	$68.65
108	$120	7.36%	$63.33
120	$1,120	7.48%	$544.62
		Price	$1,333.43
		Yield	7.65%

PROBLEM 7C

What is the price and YTM of a 5-year A rated 5% eurobond that trades at a spread of 45 basis points to the zero curve?

ANSWER:

Calculate the five discount rates. Add 45 basis points to each rate. Calculate the price and yield.

	Months	Cash Flow	Yield	+ Spread	Price
1	12	$50	4.94%	5.39%	$47.44
2	24	$50	5.71%	6.16%	$44.37
3	36	$50	6.15%	6.60%	$41.27
4	48	$50	6.47%	6.92%	$38.26
5	60	$1,050	6.71%	7.16%	$742.93
				Price	$914.28
				Yield	7.1%

PROBLEM 7D

What is bond's yield spread so the AAA zero curve of a 10-year 10% BBB bond is priced at $922.50?

ANSWER:

In this problem, you need to work backwards to determine the correct spread. Starting with the data listed in the table that follows, you need to determine the spread to add to the AAA yields so that the resulting present values sum to $922.50. This is an iterative (trial and error) process.

	ADD Spread		0	
Months	Cash Flow	AAA Yield	BBB Yield	Price
12	$100	4.94%	4.94%	$95.29
24	$100	5.71%	5.71%	$89.50
36	$100	6.15%	6.15%	$83.60
48	$100	6.47%	6.47%	$77.82
60	$100	6.71%	6.71%	$72.26
72	$100	6.91%	6.91%	$66.96
84	$100	7.08%	7.08%	$61.93
96	$100	7.23%	7.23%	$57.21
108	$100	7.36%	7.36%	$52.77
120	$1,100	7.48%	7.48%	$534.89
			Price	$1,192.23
		Price Should Equal		$922.50

By adding 4.1449% to each zero rate, the sum of the present values is $922.50:

Months	Cash Flow	Yield	Add 4.1449%	Price
12	$100	4.94%	9.09%	$91.67
24	$100	5.71%	9.85%	$82.87
36	$100	6.15%	10.30%	$74.53
48	$100	6.47%	10.61%	$66.80
60	$100	6.71%	10.86%	$59.72
72	$100	6.91%	11.06%	$53.29
84	$100	7.08%	11.23%	$47.48
96	$100	7.23%	11.38%	$42.24
108	$100	7.36%	11.51%	$37.53
120	$1,100	7.48%	11.62%	$366.38
			Price	$922.50
			Equal	$922.50

CHAPTER EIGHT

Impact of Nonparallel Yield Curve Shifts

The vast majority of the time, the yield curve does not rise or fall in parallel. If they did, all spot rates along the curve would change by the same number of basis points at the same time, and you would see a yield curve that looks like the curve shown in Figure 8.1.

FIGURE 8.1

Parallel Yield Curve Shift

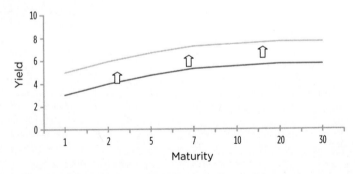

Instead, long-term rates may rise faster than short-term rates or long-term rates may fall while short-term rates are rising. Consider the 10-year 10% eurobond depicted in Figure 8.2. Suppose the current spot rates are as listed in row 3. The present value of the cash flows would be as listed in row 4. The sum of the PV of the cash flows is $1,153.67, which would be the current value of the bond. If interest rates rise by 1% all along the curve, then the present value of the cash flows will decrease to the values listed in row 5. The new value of the bond would be sum of the new PVs, or $1,083.66. Thus, if rates rise by 1%, the value of the bond would decline by $70.01. The sixth row shows the impact of a 1% rate change on each cash flow. Naturally, it also totals to $70.01.

Suppose, however, that the yield curve flattens as short-term rates rise and long-term rates fall, as depicted in Figure 8.3.

FIGURE 8.2

Bond as a Collection of Zero Coupon Bonds

	1	2	3	4	5	6	7	8	9	10
Payment	$100	$100	$100	$100	$100	$100	$100	$100	$100	$1,100
Discount	3%	4%	5%	5.8%	6.5%	7.1%	7.6%	8%	8.2%	8.3%
PV	$97.09	$92.46	$86.38	$79.81	$72.99	$66.26	$59.88	$54.03	$49.20	$495.57
PV + 1%	$96.15	$90.70	$83.96	$76.86	$69.66	$62.67	$56.13	$50.19	$45.29	$452.05
Impact	$0.94	$1.76	$2.42	$2.95	$3.33	$3.59	$3.75	$3.84	$3.91	$43.52

FIGURE 8.3

Calculating Expected Price Change for Change in Yield Curve

Year	1	2	3	4	5	6	7	8	9	10
Impact	$0.94	$1.76	$2.42	$2.95	$3.33	$3.59	$3.75	$3.84	$3.91	$43.52
% Change	-1.5%	-1.0%	-.5%	0%	0%	0%	0%	1.0%	1.5%	2.0%
$ Change	($1.41)	($1.76)	($1.21)	$0.00	$0.00	$0.00	$0.00	$3.84	$5.87	$87.04
							Total Change			$92.37

CHAPTER NINE

Interest Rate and Reinvestment Risks

Bond portfolios can be divided into two categories:

- Portfolios where the investor reinvests
- Portfolios where the investor distributes (lives on) the interest

If the investor is living on the income, the goal is to maximize the portfolio's long-term current return. For a portfolio where the investor reinvests the cash flows, managing interest rate risk becomes a more complex exercise.

When the interest payments are being reinvested, the total return in dollars (T$R) that you earn from owning a bond or bond portfolio is the sum of the three components of return that a bond offers, namely:

$$T\$R = MV + I + IOI$$

Where:

- Market Value (MV) is the current market value of the bond, which can be more or less than par and will fluctuate with changes in interest rates and credit quality.
- Interest (I) is the total interest that the portfolio has paid since you bought the bond.
- Interest on Interest (IOI) is the amount of interest you earn by reinvesting the interest payments (as well as any principal payments) you receive. This is the component of return that investors too often overlook despite the fact that it is sometimes the largest of the three components of the total return.

Every change in market interest rates impacts two components of the T$R—the MV of the bond and the IOI. If interest rates rise, the market value of the bond declines, but the amount of interest on interest that the investor earns rises.

The MV declines because, as interest rates rise, the market value of the bond must decline in order to offer a competitive yield to maturity. No one is going to pay full value for a bond that pays 6% if new bonds being issued are offering 8%. The IOI rises because as market interest rates rise, the rate at which the interest payments that are received can be reinvested also increases. If interest rates decline, the reverse happens and the MV rises, while the amount of IOI that the investor can expect to earn declines. Thus, any change in rates has a yin-yang impact on MV and IOI.

While any change in market interest rates will cause a change in the MV and IOI, a change in market interest rates does not impact both components of return to the same degree over the same time frame. Let's look at the change in MV and IOI in greater detail—starting first with the impact of a change in interest rates on the bond's market value.

INTEREST RATE IMPACT ON MARKET VALUE

When interest rates change, the market value of bonds reacts immediately. As time passes, however, the change in market value that results from a change in interest rates—either positive or negative—is mitigated because the bond accretes toward par. Thus, the change in a bond's market value (ΔMV) is maximized immediately after market interest rates change—and is mitigated by the passage of time. At maturity, any loss or gain is eliminated because the bond matures at par, as shown in Figure 9.1.

FIGURE 9.1

Change in MV vs. Time Resulting from an Instantaneous Rise in Rates from 10% to 12% on a Bond with a 10% Coupon

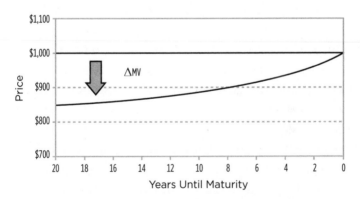

Likewise, when interest rates decline, the bond's MV rises immediately—but this rise is also mitigated by the passage of time, as shown in Figure 9.2. At maturity, any gain stemming from a decline in rates is lost because the bond matures at par.

FIGURE 9.2

Change in Market Value vs. Time from a Single Instantaneous Decline in Market Interest Rates

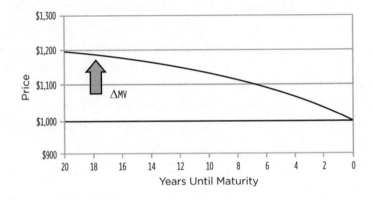

INTEREST RATE IMPACT ON INTEREST ON INTEREST

A change in market interest rates has the opposite effect on the change in the amount interest on interest ΔIOI. Unlike the change in market value that happens immediately and gets smaller as time passes, the ΔIOI happens slowly and becomes larger as time passes.

You only start to earn interest on interest after you receive your first interest payment. The difference between the amount of IOI that you originally expected to earn and the amount of IOI that is earned after rates rise is the ΔIOI. As time passes, you receive and reinvest more interest payments, and the magnitude of the ΔIOI increases. The ΔIOI increases as time passes and reaches its maximum value at maturity, as shown in Figure 9.3. Figure 9.4 summarizes the relationship between ΔMV and ΔIOI.

FIGURE 9.3

IOI for a 20-Year 10% Bond Assuming 8%, 10%, and 12% Reinvestment Rates

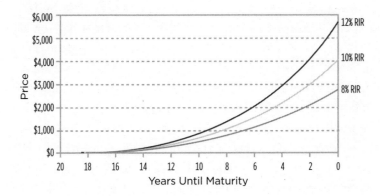

FIGURE 9.4

Summarizing the ΔMV vs. the ΔIOI

Change	Maximum Value	Passage of Time
ΔMV	Immediately	Mitigates
ΔIOI	At Maturity	Exacerbates

It should be obvious that, over a short investment horizon, ΔMV will be greater than ΔIOI. Since the ΔMV lowers your T$R when rates rise, over a short time frame your actual total dollar return (TR_{ACT}$) declines relative to the T$R you originally expected (TR_{EXP}$) if market interest rates remain unchanged. In other words, in a rising rate environment, your TR_{ACT}$ is lower than your TR_{EXP}$—provided your investment horizon is short. However, as your investment horizon increases, any negative impact of ΔMV decreases and any positive impact of ΔIOI increases. Since, as time passes, the ΔIOI increases and the ΔMV decreases, eventually your T\$R$_{ACT}$ will be greater than T\$R$_{EXP}$. Thus, given a long enough time frame, you actually benefit from a rise in market interest rates.

It stands to reason that, if over a short-term time horizon, the T\$R$_{ACT}$ is less than T\$R$_{EXP}$, and if, over a long time horizon, the T\$R$_{ACT}$ is greater than T\$R$_{EXP}$, there must be some point along the bond's life where the T\$R$_{ACT}$ equals T\$R$_{EXP}$ despite a change in market interest rates. This point is defined as the bond's duration point. Since at the duration point the change in interest rates has no impact on the investor's T\$R, the bond effectively hedges itself at its duration point. Thus, at the duration point the investor earns the YTM the investor originally expected, despite the subsequent change in market interest rates, as shown in Figure 9.5.

FIGURE 9.5
ΔMV vs. ΔIOI over Time

Pre-duration	ΔMV > ΔIOI	T\$R$_{ACT}$ < T\$R$_{EXP}$
Duration	ΔMV = ΔIOI	T\$R$_{ACT}$ = T\$R$_{EXP}$
Post-duration	ΔMV < ΔIOI	T\$R$_{ACT}$ > T\$R$_{EXP}$

If we were to graph the T\$R of a 10% 20-year bond and assume that rates fall to 8% and rise to 12%, the curves would look like the ones illustrated in Figure 9.6.

FIGURE 9.6

T$R of a 10% 20-Year Bond Assuming 2% Rate Changes

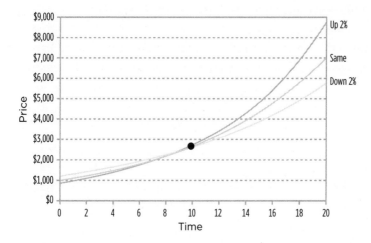

Investors have to be realistic about their level of patience. If interest rates go up, bond prices fall, and investors have a tendency to panic and sell. One key to being a successful investor is being able to stay the course. Duration tells investors how much patience they will need. As shown in Figure 9.6, if rates rise, it will take an investor 9 years of reinvesting at the higher rate for the portfolio to catch up with its original projected value. Does the investor have 9 years of patience? If not, the investor should shorten the portfolio to the point where they are comfortable. If an investor is only willing to wait 3 years to catch up with its original projected value, the investor should have a portfolio that has a duration of 3 years.

This brings us to the second definition of duration: Duration is the point along a bond's life where risk is minimized.

In most strategic asset allocation models, we define risk as the uncertainty of return and measure it by calculating the standard deviation of the portfolio. If risk is defined this way, then a bond has the least degree of risk if it is held to its duration point. The further the holding period or investment horizon deviates from the bond's duration—in either direction—the greater the uncertainty of return and, therefore, the greater the risk.

Conversely, traders who hold bonds for very short periods of time and investors who hold bonds until they mature have the greatest degree of uncertainty with regards to their return. At these extremely short and long time investment horizons, interest rate risk and reinvestment risk have no opportunity to offset each other—and risk is maximized, as Figure 9.7 shows.

FIGURE 9.7

T$R of a 10% 20-Year Bond Assuming 2% Rate Changes

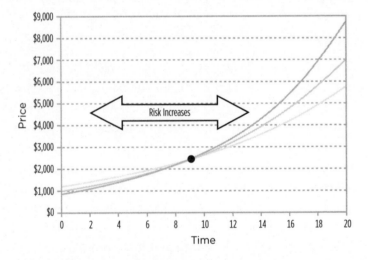

Following this same line of logic leads us to the third definition of duration: Duration is the point in a bond's life where an investor who reinvests actually earns the bond's YTM.

For investors who reinvest, the YTM isn't the return they'll earn if the bond is held to maturity. The reason is that each interest payment that is received is reinvested—and the rate at which it will be reinvested is dependent upon interest rate changes during the time the investor owns the bond. Figure 9.8 shows the assumed shape of the yield curve.

FIGURE 9.8

Assumed Shape of the Yield Curve in the YTM Calculation of a Bond Offering an 8% YTM

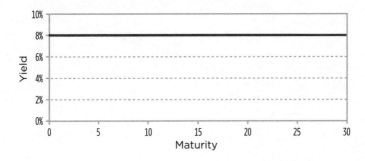

The only point in a bond's life when an investor can reasonably anticipate earning the YTM is if the investor holds the bond to its duration point. Figure 9.9 shows the YTM for reinvestors at duration and at maturity.

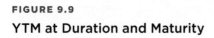

FIGURE 9.9

YTM at Duration and Maturity

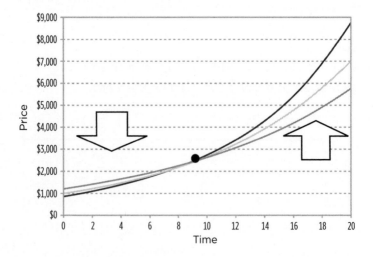

The reason an investor earns the YTM at the duration point and the reason why the ΔMV and the ΔIOI offset each other at the duration point provides the 4th definition of duration: Duration is the point in a bond's life where an investor receives half of the present value of the bond's future cash flows.

Consider that for reinvestors the duration point is both:

- The point where the two risks (interest rate risk and reinvestment risk) balance
- The point where reinvestors actually earn the YTM.

Now, it makes sense that the duration point would be the point in a bond's life where an investor receives half of the present value the bond's future cash flows—with the second half still to come.

In order to calculate where this point is, we need to review two concepts:

- The time-weighting of future cash flows
- The discounting of future cash flows

Time-Weighting Future Cash Flows

Starting with time-weighting, consider the following two cash flows:

Payable in 1 year(s): $100
Payable in 2 year(s): $100

If you want to determine when (on average) monies are received, time-weight the cash flows by the times when they are received:

$1 \times \$100 = \$100$
$2 \times \underline{\$100} = \underline{\$200}$
Total (unweighted) = $200
Total (time-weighted) = $300

$$\frac{\$300 \text{ Total Time-Weighted Cash Flows}}{\$200 \text{ Total Cash Flows}}$$

Now, reduce the equation and eliminate cash flow from both the numerator and denominator:

$300 / $200 = 1.5 years

In other words, reinvestors receive their money (on average) in 1.5 years.

PROBLEM 9A

Now, consider these three cash flows:

Payable in 1 year(s): $100
Payable in 2 year(s): $100
Payable in 3 year(s): $100

ANSWER:

To determine when (on average) reinvestors receive their money, time-weight the cash flows as follows:

$1 \times \$100 = \$100$
$2 \times \$100 = \$200$
$3 \times \underline{\$100} = \underline{\$300}$
Total cash flows = $300
Total time-weighted cash flows = $600

$$\frac{\$600 \text{ Total Time-Weighted Cash Flows}}{\$300 \text{ Total Cash Flows}}$$

$600 / $300 = 2 years

In other words, reinvestors receive their money (on average) in 2 years.

PROBLEM 9B

Now, consider these next three unequal cash flows:

Payable in 1 year(s): $300
Payable in 2 year(s): $100
Payable in 3 year(s): $600

ANSWER:

To determine when (on average) reinvestors receive their money, time-weight the cash flows as follows:

$1 \times \$300 = \$300$
$2 \times \$100 = \$200$
$3 \times \underline{\$600} = \underline{\$1,800}$
Total (unweighted) = $1,000
Total (time-weighted) = $2,300

$$\frac{\$2,300 \text{ Total Time-Weighted Cash Flows}}{\$1,000 \text{ Total Cash Flows}}$$

$2,300 / $1,000 = 2.3 years

Even though they receive the money over 3 years, since the bulk of it comes at the end of the third year, on average reinvestors receive it in 2.3 years.

PROBLEM 9C

Consider the cash flow schedule of the 10% 6-year eurobond shown in Figure 9. 10. (Note: Eurobonds only pay interest once per year.)

Payable in 1 year(s): $100
Payable in 2 year(s): $100
Payable in 3 year(s): $100
Payable in 4 year(s): $100
Payable in 5 year(s): $100
Payable in 6 year(s): $1,100

FIGURE 9.10

The Cash Flows of a 6% 10-Year Eurobond

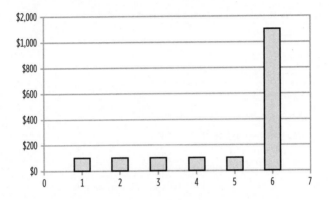

Determine when, on average, we receive our money.

ANSWER:

Time-weight the cash flows as follows:

$1 \times \$100 = \$100$
$2 \times \$100 = \$200$
$3 \times \$100 = \$300$
$4 \times \$100 = \$400$
$5 \times \$100 = \$500$
$6 \times \underline{\$1,100} = \underline{\$6,600}$
Total cash flow = $1,600
Total time-weighted cash flow = $8,100

$$\frac{\$8,100 \text{ Time-Weighted Cash Flows}}{\$1,600 \text{ Total Cash Flows}}$$

$8,100 / $1,600 = 5.06 years

Time-Discounting Future Cash Flows

Now that we have reviewed time-weighting, let's turn our attention to discounting. Future cash flows are discounted because a dollar received today is more valuable than a dollar received in the future; a dollar received today can be reinvested. The longer an investor has to wait to receive money, the less valuable it becomes.

For the 6-year 10% eurobond described in Problem 9C and priced at par, the present value of each future cash flow can be found by discounting it by the bond's YTM. Since the bond is trading at par, its coupon and YTM are the same—that is 10%.

If we discount each cash flow at 10% using the formula depicted in Figure 9.11, then the present values would be as depicted in Figure 9.12 and Figure 9.13.

FIGURE 9.11

PV Formula

$$PV = \frac{FV}{(1+r)^n}$$

FIGURE 9.12

The Present Values

Year	Cash Flow	PV
1	$100	$90.91
2	$100	$82.64
3	$100	$75.13
4	$100	$68.30
5	$100	$62.09
6	$1,100	$620.92

FIGURE 9.13

Present Value of the Cash Flows

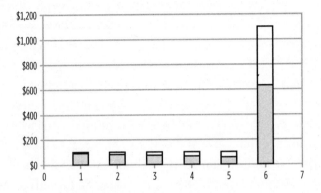

If we then time-weight the PV of the cash flows, the result is 4.79 years.

Year	Cash Flow	PV	Time Weighted
1	$100	$90.91	$90.91
2	$100	$82.64	$165.29
3	$100	$75.13	$225.39
4	$100	$68.30	$273.21
5	$100	$62.09	$310.46
6	$1,100	$620.92	$3,725.53
Totals		$1,000.00	$4,790.79

Duration = $4,790.79 / $1,000.00 = 4.79 years

In other words, in 4.79 years you will have received half of the bond's value (adjusted for time) with half still to come, as shown in Figure 9.14.

FIGURE 9.14

Balance Point of the Time-Weighted Future Cash Flows

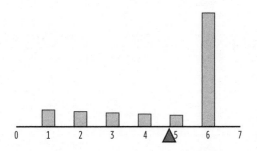

As we defined before, this time-weighted present value of the cash flows is the bond's duration—often referred to as "Macaulay's duration." It is called Macaulay's duration because Frederick Macaulay was the first person to publish work on duration. It is at the duration point where the various T$R curves intersect.

As some additional illustrative examples, let's calculate the duration of some bonds:

- An 8% 4-year US Corporate Bond priced at 106½
- A 15-year Treasury zero coupon bond priced to offer a 9% return
- A US Treasury 15%-July-15-2012 as of 3/3/01; assume the bond is priced to offer a 10.45% return

PROBLEM 9D

Calculate the duration of the 8% 4-year US Corporate Bond at 106½.

ANSWER:

Because this bond pays interest semiannually, it generates eight cash flows. To calculate its duration, first calculate duration in periods, and then convert it to duration in years. The discount rate is the YTM per period.

Year	Cash Flow	PV	Time Weighted
1	40	$38.81	$38.81
2	40	$37.65	$75.30
3	40	$36.53	$109.59
4	40	$35.44	$141.77
5	40	$34.39	$171.93
6	40	$33.36	$200.16
7	40	$32.37	$226.57
8	1,040	$816.46	$6,531.65
		$1,065.00	$7,495.77

$7,495.77 Total Time-Weighted Cash Flow
$1,065.00 Sum of PV of Cash Flows

$7,495.77 / $1,065.00 = 7.038 Duration in periods

To convert duration in periods to duration in years, which is how duration is typically expressed, divide the duration in periods by the number of periods per year. In this problem:

Duration in years = 7.038 / 2 payments per year = 3.519

Alternatively, the same duration can be calculated using the duration function in Excel.

To use the duration function in Excel, first make sure that the Analysis ToolPak is activated. To do so, simply check Analysis ToolPak, which can be found under Tools > Add-Ins. Then, in any cell, paste the function by selecting Insert > Function > Financial > Duration. This brings up the dialog box shown in Figure 9.15.

FIGURE 9.15

Microsoft Excel Duration Function Dialog Box

Duration

Settlement _____

Maturity   _____

Coupon   _____

Yield   _____

Frequency   _____

Returns the annual duration of a security with periodic interest payments

Settlement

Formula Result =

In the Settlement text box, enter the settlement date inside a set of quotation marks: "MM/DD/YYYY". Alternatively, enter address of the cell that contains the settlement date or the current date, if the bond is already owned.

In the Maturity text box, enter the maturity date inside a set of quotation marks "MM/DD/YYYY" or enter the address of the cell that contains the maturity date.

In the Coupon text box, enter the bond's annual coupon. (A 7.25% coupon would be entered as .0725.) Alternatively, you can enter the address of the cell that contains the coupon.

In the Yield text box, enter the current YTM to at least two decimal places. (A YTM of 11.33% would be entered as .1133.) Alternatively, you can enter the address of the cell that contains the coupon.

In the Frequency text box, enter the number of periods per year, typically 1 for eurobonds and 2 for US bonds.

Scroll down to the last text box: Calendar basis. For all US bonds except Treasuries enter 0—which means a 30/360 calendar. For Treasuries enter 1. When you are finished, click OK to save the settings and close the dialog box.

The duration is then displayed in the cell. Click the boxed question mark if you have any questions. Clicking this question mark brings up the Help screens.

PROBLEM 9E

Calculate the duration of a 15-year Treasury zero coupon bond priced to offer a 9% return.

ANSWER:

Since this is a zero coupon bond, there is only one cash flow. Even though there is only one cash flow, the convention is still to calculate and express the yield as if the bond compounds semiannually. Thus, the table we use to calculate duration would be as shown in Figure 9.16.

FIGURE 9.16

Cash Flow Table for Zero Coupon Bond

Number	Cash Flow	PV	Time Weighted
1	0	$0.00	$0
2-29	0	$0.00	$0
30	1,000	$267.00	$8,010
Totals		$267.00	$8,010

Time-Weighted $8,010 / $267 = Duration in 30 periods

30 periods / 2 periods per year = Duration in 15 years

For zero coupon bonds, duration equals maturity. This makes sense; there is no ΔIOI to offset the change in ΔMV.

PROBLEM 9F

Calculate the duration of a US Treasury 15%-July-15-2012 as of 3/3/01. Assume the bond is priced to offer a 10.45% return.

ANSWER:

In this example, the bond doesn't mature in a whole number of periods. Therefore, our duration calculation has to take partial periods and accrued interest into account. While we could set up a table based on partial periods, it is much easier to use the duration function in Excel.

Settlement	"3/03/2001"
Maturity	"7/15/2012"
Coupon	.15
Yield	.1045
Frequency	2
Basis	1
Result	**6.63**

(Note: Result is already adjusted to be expressed annually.)

CHAPTER TEN

Variables That Impact Duration

Now that I've illustrated how duration is calculated, let's examine the six main factors that impact a bond's duration. These include:

- Size of the coupon
- Maturity of the bond
- Yield to maturity
- Tax rate
- Actual payment of interest
- Impact of embedded options

Let's look at each of these factors in some detail.

SIZE OF THE COUPON

All other factors being equal, the lower the bond's coupon, the higher its duration. Logically, this makes sense. Lower coupon payments mean less cash flow that can be reinvested at a new rate per year. This extends the time it takes before the ΔIOI can offset the ΔMV.

Consider the following example. Suppose you own two 20-year bonds, one with a 2% coupon and the other with an 18% coupon. Both bonds are priced to offer a 10% YTM. Naturally, the bond with an 18% coupon will be priced at a substantial premium, while the one with a 2% coupon will be priced at a substantial discount.

If market interest rates rise by 1%, the value of both bonds will decline. But, they won't decline by equal percentages. The low coupon bond declines by 12.85%, while the high coupon bond declines by 7.99%.

MV of 2% 20-year bond priced to offer 10% YTM = $313.64

MV of 2% 20-year bond priced to offer 11% YTM
  = $277.92 (loss of 12.85%)

MV of 18% 20-year bond priced to offer 10% YTM
  = $1,696.36

MV of 18% 20-year bond priced to offer 11% YTM
  = $1,561.61 (loss of 7.99%)

The higher the coupon, the smaller the loss—in percentage terms. In addition, over time, this decline is offset by the increases in the amount of interest on interest that can be earned by reinvesting the coupons at the new 11% rate. In the case of the 2% bond, only $20 per year is received and, therefore, is available to be reinvested. In the case of the 18% bond, $180 per year is received and is, therefore, available to be reinvested at the higher rate.

Obviously, it will take less time to offset a 7.99% loss when $180 per year is available for reinvestment at the higher rate than it will take to offset a 12.85% loss when only $20 per year is available for reinvestment. Because the bonds with high coupons can make up a loss so quickly, they are frequently referred to as cushion bonds because investors who own them are cushioned against a rise in rates, as shown in Figure 10.1.

FIGURE 10.1

T$R Curves of High Coupon Bonds

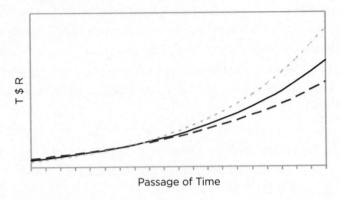

At the other extreme, the duration of zero coupon bonds is equal to their maturity because there is no cash flow to reinvest and there is never a time when the ΔIOI will offset the ΔMV. Figure 10.2 shows the T$R curves for ZCBs.

FIGURE 10.2

Total Dollar Return Curves of Zero Coupon Bonds

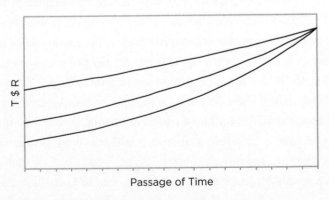

The graph shown in Figure 10.3 illustrates how altering the coupon of a 20-year eurobond priced to offer an 8% YTM impacts the bond's duration. Note that the relationship is not linear.

FIGURE 10.3

Duration of 20-Year Eurobonds with Various Coupons

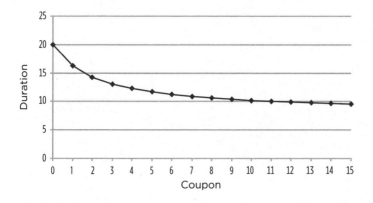

MATURITY

The second variable that impacts a bond's duration is its maturity. All other factors being equal, the longer a bond's maturity, the higher its duration. Remember the numerator in the duration calculation is found by summing the PV of each of the cash flow multiplied by its number. The denominator in the duration calculation is found by summing the PV of each cash flow. Thus, as maturity increases, the numerator increases at a faster rate than the denominator—causing the duration to rise. However, because the number of the cash flow is multiplied by the PV of the cash flows and the present value declines as maturity increases, the duration increases at an ever decreasing rate.

The graph shown in Figure 10.4 illustrates the impact of increasing the maturity of a 10% corporate bond priced at par. As the maturity increases, the duration approaches a limit. Once maturity gets past 40 years or so, the present value of any payments received further in the future is so low that they cause the impact of the payment to be negligible. For this reason, the duration of a 100-year bond is not much higher than that of a 40-year bond.

FIGURE 10.4

Duration vs. Maturity

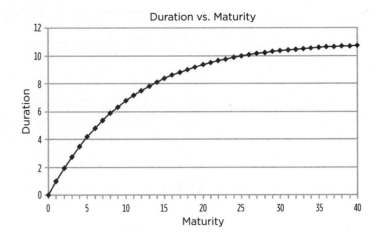

Yield to Maturity

All other factors being equal, the third variable that impacts duration is the bond's yield to maturity (YTM). As the bond's YTM changes, its duration also changes. The reason duration is a function of YTM is that in the duration calculation, the cash flows are present valued by discounting them at the YTM. As the YTM changes, so do the present values of the cash flows and, therefore, so does the duration.

As market interest rates go up, the present value of the bond's cash flows decline and, therefore, so does the bond's duration. As market interest rates go down, the present value of the cash flows and, therefore, the bond's duration declines. The change in the duration of a bond in response to a change in rates is called convexity and it is covered in detail later in this book.

The graph shown in Figure 10.5 illustrates how the duration of a 30-year 10% coupon eurobond is impacted by changing its YTM.

FIGURE 10.5

Duration vs. Yield

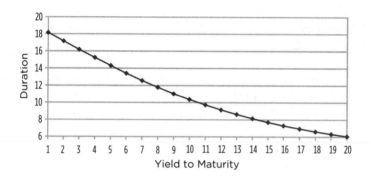

TAXES

The fourth variable that impacts a bond's duration is taxes. Just as is the case with YTM, dealers and newspapers quote duration on a pre-tax basis and leave it to investors to account for the impact of taxes. The tax rate that's applied to the bond's interest payments and capital gains or losses is dependent upon both the type of bond and the type of investor. For example, a US corporate bond owned in a pension account would be tax free, while the same bond owned by an individual would be fully taxable.

All other factors being equal, as the effective tax rate on a bond increases, a bond's duration also increases. An increase in the tax rate increases the bond's duration because it effectively lowers the amount of cash that can be reinvested. Unfortunately, some investors and fixed income portfolio managers ignore the impact of taxes when they calculate duration.

As the effective tax rate rises, so does the duration of the bond because the cash flow is reduced.

Figure 10.6 shows the impact of taxes on the duration calculation of an 8% 4-year eurobond priced at par. Assume that the investor is subject to a 50% tax rate.

FIGURE 10.6

Impact of Taxes

Year	Pre-Tax Cash Flow	After-Tax Cash Flow	PV of After-Tax Cash Flow	Time-Weighted Cash Flow
1	$80	$40	$38.46	$38.46
2	$80	$40	$36.98	$73.96
3	$80	$40	$35.56	$106.68
4	$1,080	$1,040	$899	$3,555.99
	Total time-weighted cash flows			$3,775.09
	Market value of the bond			$1,000
	After-tax duration			3.78

In the case of zero coupon bonds, when they are held in taxable accounts by investors subject to taxation, the duration actually exceeds the maturity. The reason is that the cash flows in the years prior to maturity are negative because investors have to pay taxes on cash flows they haven't yet received.

Impact of Coupon Payment

The fifth factor that impacts a bond's duration is the payment of interest. In between interest payment dates, the duration of a bond decreases in a linear manner. When a bond makes an interest payment, the duration of the bond rises because the short-term cash flow is no longer part of the weighted average. Consider the following example that illustrates the concept. Suppose there's a bond with three remaining cash flows:

0 Years and 1 Day	$100
1 Year and 1 Day	$100
2 Years and 1 Day	$100

In this case, the weighted average of when the cash flows are received is a year and a day. One day later when the coupon is paid, the remaining cash flows would be:

1 Year	$100
2 Years	$100

The weighted average is now 1.5 years. Because the short-term cash flow is no longer part of the average, the average is longer. Thus, as the bond approaches maturity, its duration declines in a jagged nonlinear path, as shown in Figure 10.7.

FIGURE 10.7

Impact of Interest Payments on Duration

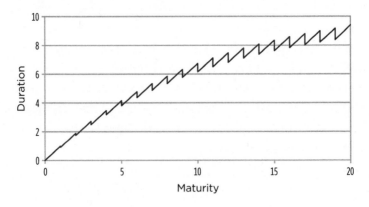

IMPACT OF EMBEDDED OPTIONS

The sixth variable that impacts a bond's duration is embedded options. A bond that is callable or putable will have a different duration depending upon whether or not the bond is called, put, or survives until maturity. There are two ways to account for embedded options when calculating duration.

The simple, although less accurate, way is to determine whether it is currently attractive to exercise the option. If it is, then assume that the option will be exercised and calculate the duration to the date the option is exercised. If it is not, then calculate the duration to the maturity date.

Consider the following example: Suppose there is a bond that matures in 15 years but is callable in 5 years at a price of $1,030. If the bond is currently selling at a price higher than $1,030, assume the bond will be called, calculate the duration to the call date, and assume that the last cash flow will be $1,030 plus the last interest payment. If the bond is selling for less than $1,030, calculate the duration of the bond to the maturity date.

While that approximate method is certainly easy, it is not especially accurate. Just because the bond is selling above or below $1,030 today doesn't mean that it will stay there when the bond can actually be called.

The more accurate method is to determine the probability that the bond will be called and the probability that it won't be called. Then, take the weighted average of the two alternatives to determine the bond's most probable life. Once the most probable life is determined, the duration can be calculated to this life. This methodology, as well as other aspects of embedded options, is described in the section on option adjusted spreads.

DURATION IS A MOVING TARGET

As you can see, a bond's duration is a function of coupon maturity, YTM, taxes, and the value of embedded options. Since these all change as time passes, so does a bond's duration. The bond's duration point is always a point in the future that you can never reach until the bond matures or is called or put.

Several strategies require matching the duration of a portfolio of bonds to the duration of a pool of liabilities. Because the durations of the assets and liabilities might change at different rates, it is often necessary to rebalance the portfolio to bring the durations back into balance.

DURATION OF ALTERNATIVE DEBT INSTRUMENTS

In the previous sections, calculating the duration of traditional fixed rate notes and bonds was discussed. It is also important to understand how to calculate the duration of nontraditional fixed income instruments. While the calculations are not difficult, it is necessary to think creatively in order to calculate the duration of nontraditional instruments. Examples using floating rate notes, preferred stocks, and interest rate swaps will illustrate.

Floating Rate Notes

Floating rate notes (FRN) are notes with an interest rate that periodically resets to the prevailing market rate as defined by an index. For example, a 5-year FRN might pay US$ LIBOR plus 50 basis points with a 6-month reset. Calculating its duration poses an interesting dilemma because the cash flows are uncertain. There are several alternative methodologies that can be used to calculate the duration of an FRN. The decision of which method to use depends on whether or not the investor expects the FRN to reset at par at its next reset date.

If an assumption is made that the floating rate note has characteristics that will enable it to reset to par on its next reset date, then the note's duration will equal the time to the next reset date. If the note's coupon resets in 6 months, the duration of the note is 6 months. One month later the same note's duration is 5 months. The day before the note resets its duration will be one day, and on the reset day the duration will again be 6 months.

However, if an assumption is made that the note will not reset at par (either because the note's credit was downgraded or for some other reason), then the duration calculation becomes more complex. Because the note will not reset at par, the only way that the duration of the note can be calculated is to first swap the floating rate cash flows for fixed rate cash flows. The fixed rate cash flows that are the equivalent of the floating rate cash flows can be determined via the swap market. Once the equivalent fixed rate cash flows are determined, the duration of the fixed rate cash flows can be calculated using the traditional duration calculation.

Many investors buy FRNs because they believe that FRNs have very low durations and will lower the durations of their portfolios. Unfortunately, unless the FRNs reset at par, their durations can extend substantially. In this circumstance, instead of shortening the portfolio's duration, the FRNs increase the portfolio's duration.

PREFERRED STOCKS

Preferred stocks pose another interesting problem. Equity is perpetual—and therefore a non-putable preferred stock could theoretically pay dividends forever. Because of this infinite stream of future cash flows, it first appears that the duration of a preferred stock is also infinite. Unfortunately, the obvious answer is not always the correct answer.

The reason that the duration of a preferred stock or perpetual bond is not infinite is that each successive cash flow comes further in the future. Since each cash flow comes further in the future, it has a lower present value today. Eventually the cash flows come so far in the future that their present value rounds to less than a penny. Thus, as the maturity of an instrument approached infinity, the duration reaches a limit. Mathematically, this limit is approximately (1 + yield) / yield.

For an 8% perpetual preferred priced at par, the duration would be:

$(1 + .08) / .08 = 13.5$ years

The same logic applies to perpetual debt offerings, like those occasionally issued by various European sovereign issuers.

CHAPTER ELEVEN

Modified Duration

In the last chapter, we discussed the concept of duration. Closely related to duration is the concept of modified duration. A bond's modified duration is calculated using the next formula:

Modified Duration (in Periods) = MD
= Duration (in Periods) / 1 + YTM (per Period)

A bond's modified duration is a measure of the amount of interest rate risk in a bond. Specifically, a bond's modified duration is an approximate measure of how much the value of a bond will change (in percent) if interest rates change by 1%. Figure 11.1 shows the impact on a bond of several different modified durations.

FIGURE 11.1

Modified Durations

Modified Duration	Description
6	When market interest rates change by 1%, the value of the bond will change by approximately 6%.
12	When market interest rates change by 1%, the value of the bond will change by approximately 12%.
29	When market interest rates change by 1%, the value of the bond will change by approximately 29%.

Because a bond's modified duration is calculated from its duration, we need to calculate a bond's duration first. From duration we get modified duration, which is the percentage change in price due to a 1% change in market value. From the percentage change in price we can calculate the price change in dollar terms by using the formula below:

$$\text{Gain or Loss} = \$MV \times MD \times -\Delta IR$$

Where:

- $\$MV$ = Current market value of the portfolio
- MD = Modified duration of the bond or portfolio
- $-\Delta IR$ = Change in interest rates (a negative value because a rise in rates causes a decline in price)

Investors typically measure the sensitivity of their portfolios to a single basis point change in market interest rates. A basis point is defined as one one-hundredth of a percent—or 1% of 1%. In the above equation:

- A single basis point ΔIR is entered as .0001
- A ten basis point ΔIR is entered as .001
- A one hundred basis point ΔIR (a 1% ΔIR) is entered as .01

Let us look at several examples.

PROBLEM 11A

How will the value of a bond currently selling for $945 change if interest rates rise by 50 basis points and the MD of the bond is 6.34?

ANSWER:

Loss = MV × MD × −ΔIR
Loss = $945 × 6.34 × −(.0050) = −$29.96

PROBLEM 11B

How will the value of a 100 bond position currently selling at 103½ change if interest rates fall by 35 basis points and the MD of the bond is 8.99?

ANSWER:

Gain = MV × MD × −ΔIR
Gain = ($1,035 × 100) × 8.99 × −(−.0035) = $3,256.63
(Note, the negative times a negative change in rates
    results in a positive change in price.)

PROBLEM 11C

How will the value of a portfolio change if the portfolio has a weighted average modified duration of 5.66, a market value of

$5,345,600, and the investor expects interest rates to rise by 8 basis points?

ANSWER:

Loss = MV × MD × –ΔIR
Gain = $5,345,600 × 5.66 × –(.0008) = –$24,204.88

In all of these problems, when we say that interest rates change by 1, 10, or 100 basis points, we mean that entire yield curve shifts in a parallel fashion by that number of basis points. Remember that a 20-year bond has cash flows that occur every 6 months and, therefore, its price is determined by changes in the short-, intermediate-, and long-term spot rates.

KEY RATE DURATIONS

Closely related to the concept of modified duration is the concept of key rate durations. While it is relatively easy to calculate the value of a .01 ΔIR for an entire portfolio of bonds, as noted earlier, the answer is only relevant if the yield curve is expected to shift in a parallel manner. It is often more useful to calculate how the value of a portfolio will change if certain key rates, such as the 3-month, 1-year, 3-year, 5-year, 10-year, and 30-year rates, were to each change by 1 basis point while the other rates stayed constant.

By calculating the interest rate sensitivity of the portfolio to a change in rates at specific points along the curve, it is possible to get a clearer picture of the portfolio's risk profile. For example, the market value of all three of the portfolios described in Figure 11.2 would experience the same price change to a parallel change in rates. However, they would experience very different changes in market value in response to a nonparallel change in rates.

FIGURE 11.2

Interest Rate Sensitivity of Alternative Portfolios to Changes in Different Interest Rates

	3M	1Y	3Y	5Y	10Y	30Y	Total
Port 1	$200	$200	$200	$200	$200	$200	$1,200
Port 2	$50	$150	$400	$400	$150	$50	$1,200
Port 3	$400	$150	$50	$50	$150	$400	$1,200

In the first portfolio, the interest rate risk is evenly distributed along the yield curve because a change in any of the key interest rates results in the same change to the value of the portfolio. In the second portfolio, the interest rate risk is concentrated at the 3- to 5-year point along the curve. Changes in short-term rates and long-term rates have little effect on the portfolio. In the third portfolio, the risk is concentrated at the extremes of the yield curve. If, for example, you expected the yield curve to shift in the manner depicted in Figure 11.3, you would have a clear preference for the second portfolio.

FIGURE 11.3

Expected Yield Curve Change

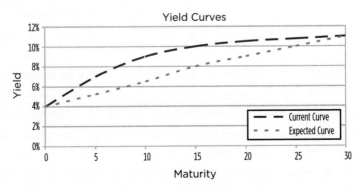

CHAPTER TWELVE

Convexity

Closely related to the concept of duration is the subject of convexity. Like duration, convexity has more than one definition:

- Convexity is the 1st derivative of the modified duration less the yield function
- Convexity is the 2nd derivative of the price less the yield function

For readers without a math background, these definitions are more than a little cryptic, so let's start by defining the term "derivative." The term "derivative" simply means "measures the change in." Thus, convexity measures the change in modified duration in response to a change in yield. Perhaps the easiest way to understand 1st and 2nd derivative functions is to illustrate them using a familiar example:

Location → Speed → Acceleration

- Speed is the 1st derivative of location since speed measures the rate at which one's location changes, such as 5 feet per second or 55 miles per hour.
- Acceleration is the 1st derivative of speed because acceleration measures the rate at which speed is changing, such as the speed increasing by 10 miles every 10 minutes.
- Since acceleration is the 1st derivative of speed and speed is, in turn, the 1st derivative of location, acceleration is the 2nd derivative of location. As the rate of acceleration changes, so will the location.

Likewise:

Price → Modified Duration → Convexity

- Modified duration (MD) is the 1st derivative of price with respect to yield because MD measures how price of a bond changes in response to a change in interest rates.
- Convexity is the 1st derivative of MD with respect to yield because convexity measures the rate at which MD changes in response to a change in interest rates.
- Since convexity is the 1st derivative of MD and MD is, in turn, the 1st derivative of price, convexity is the 2nd derivative of price. As interest rates change, convexity changes—causing MD to change—which results to price changes.

The easiest way to visualize convexity is with an example. Consider a 20.7-year 10% eurobond priced at par. This bond has a modified duration equal to 10. According to duration analysis, if the modified duration equals 10, every time market interest rates change by 1%, the market value of the bond should change by 10%.

Since the bond is priced at par, 10% of par is equal to $100. Thus, every 1% change in rates would result in a $100 change in the price of the bond. If this is true, the price/yield relationship of this bond would be as illustrated in Figure 12.1.

FIGURE 12.1

The Price Yield Function of a Bond

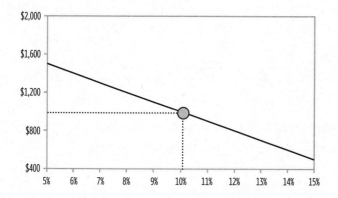

However, when we observe the actual relationship between the price and yield of this bond in the market, the relationship looks more like the pattern shown in Figure 12.2. When looked at from below, the actual relationship is not linear. Instead, the price path appears to be convex, hence the name "convexity" (as shown in Figure 12.2).

The first question we need to answer then is, "Why is the price-yield relationship for this bond convex?"

FIGURE 12.2

Positive Convexity

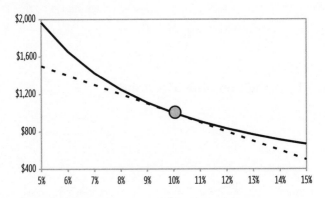

The reason is that the value of a .01 ΔIR changes as interest rates change. Initially the value of a .01 ΔIR is equal to:

MV × MD × .0001 = Value .01 ΔIR
$1,000 × 10 × .0001 = $1

However, as interest rates change, both the market value and the modified duration change. For example, as interest rates rise, both the MD and MV decline—lowering the value of a .01 ΔIR.

MV × MD × .0001 = Value .01 ΔIR
↓ × ↓ × .0001 =   ↓

As interest rates continue to rise, the value of a .01 ΔIR continues to decline and each successive increase in rates results in a smaller loss of MV. Likewise, as market interest rates decline, the modified duration and the value of a .01 ΔIR increase. Thus, as interest rates continue to decline, the resulting increase in the market value becomes progressively greater.

Given the choice between investing in a bond that has a linear price yield relationship or one with a convex price yield relationship, any investor would prefer the bond with the convex path—all other factors being equal. After all, the convex line results in smaller losses and larger gains from symmetric interest rate changes. Since this bond's price convexity benefits the investor regardless of whether rates rise or fall, this bond exhibits positive convexity in both directions.

All bullet bonds exhibit positive convexity. Their durations extend when rates decline and their durations shorten when rates rise—just what an investor would do when actively managing the portfolio. Of course, not all bonds are bullet bonds, and not all bonds exhibit positive convexity.

For example, consider a pool of current coupon mortgages. When interest rates decline, investors normally want to increase the duration of their portfolios in order to increase their gains. However, as market interest rates decline, an increasing percentage of the homeowners in the pool refinance their mortgages. Refinancing shortens the mortgage pool's duration. Thus, instead of getting progressively larger gains as interest rates decline, investors in current coupon mortgages get progressively smaller gains as rates decline.

Likewise, when interest rates rise, investors normally try to shorten the duration of their portfolios in order to minimize their losses. However, when rates rise, the duration of a pool of mortgages often extends because fewer people can afford to move up to larger homes or take new jobs that require relocating. Thus the duration of the pool gets longer just when the investor wants it to get shorter.

Since the duration of a pool of mortgage changes in the opposite way investors would choose, pools of current coupon mortgages exhibit negative convexity, as shown in Figure 12.3. (Note that not all mortgage pools exhibit negative convexity—but that current coupon mortgages generally do.)

FIGURE 12.3

Price Yield of Current Coupon Mortgage Pool

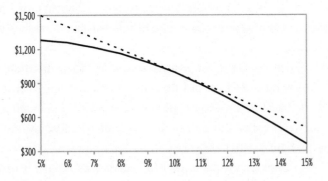

Some bonds exhibit positive convexity when rates change in one direction but not when they move in the other direction. Consider the case of a 10-bond that is currently priced at par, is callable at par in 2 years, but matures in 10 years. This bond's remaining life will either be 2 years or 10 years, depending on whether the bond is called.

As interest rates rise, the probability increases that the bond will last 10 years. As interest rates decline, the probability increases that the bond will only last 2 years. As the projected maturity of the bond changes, so does its projected duration. As interest rates decrease, the bonds expected life and duration decrease, which is the opposite of what the investor would desire. As interest rates rise, the bonds expected life and duration extend—again to the detriment of the investor. Thus, this callable bond exhibits negative convexity along a long portion of the price yield relationship. A callable bond will exhibit positive convexity only if interest rates rise to the point where the embedded option becomes valueless, or rates fall to the point where having the bond called is a virtual certainty.

Clearly, from the investor's point of view, positive convexity is a very desirable characteristic for an investment to have. Unfortunately, like any other desirable characteristic, such as high credit quality or liquidity, positive convexity has to be purchased. It is purchased by accepting a lower yield from bonds that exhibit positive convexity than from those bonds that exhibit negative convexity. An instrument with positive price convexity will yield less than an instrument with neutral or negative convexity—all other factors being equal.

To perform the type of "what-if" analysis discussed in the last section, it is necessary to calculate a bond's convexity and then determine how much of an impact the bond's convexity will have on the bond's price. The next equation is used to calculate the modified convexity of a bullet bond:

$$\text{Modified Convexity} = \sum_{1}^{n} \frac{n(n+1)PV(CFn)}{PV(PPY)^{PPY}} \times \frac{1}{\left[1 + \dfrac{YTM}{PPY}\right]^{PPY}}$$

Figure 12.4 illustrates the calculation of the modified convexity of a 10% 10-year eurobond priced at par.

FIGURE 12.4

Calculating Modified Convexity

Cash Flow Number	Cash Flow Amount	PV of Cash Flow	n(n + 1)	Column (3 × 4)
1	$100	$90.91	2	$181.82
2	$100	$82.64	6	$495.84

Cash Flow Number	Cash Flow Amount	PV of Cash Flow	n(n + 1)	Column (3 × 4)
3	$100	$75.13	12	$901.56
4	$100	$68.30	20	$1,366.00
5	$100	$62.09	30	$1,862.70
6	$100	$56.45	42	$2,370.90
7	$100	$51.32	56	$2,873.92
8	$100	$46.65	72	$3,358.80
9	$100	$42.41	90	$3,816.90
10	$1,100	$424.10	110	$46,651.00
Sum of the last column				$63,879.44
Divided by MV(PPY)^2 = $1,000(1)^2				638.79
Multiply by 1 / (1 + YTM / PPY)^{PPY} = 1 / (1 + .1 / 1)^1				1 / 1.1
Convexity				58.07

Once the convexity (C) is calculated, it can be used to calculate the expected price change of a bond due to a change in rates. The formula for the price change expressed as a percentage is:

$$\Delta \text{Price}(\%)_{\text{CONV}} = [.5 \times C \times (\Delta \text{YTM})^2]$$

For example, if interest rates were to change by 150 basis points, the value of the 10-year 10% eurobond would change by 0.653% as a result of its convexity.

$$\Delta \text{Price}(\%)_{\text{CONV}} = [.5 \times 58.07 \times (.0150)^2] = .00653 = 0.653\%$$

Note, that since this is 2nd derivative function, the change in yields is squared. Since it is squared, it makes no difference if interest rates rise or fall since both positive and negative numbers, when squared, are positive numbers. Also, since in the price change calculation above, the yield change is squared, small changes in rates result in almost no convexity impact.

For example, for a 1bp change in rates:

$$\Delta Price(\%)_{CONV} = [.5 \times 58.07 \times (.0001)^2] = .00000029$$
$$= 0.000029\%$$

This is less than $.01 in dollar terms. For small changes in market interest rates, the impact of convexity can be safely ignored.

As with duration, the price change due to convexity can also be calculated in dollars by rearranging the equation. The formula for determining the price change of the bond (expressed in dollars) in response to a change in rates as a result of convexity is:

$$\Delta Price(\$)_{CONV} = [.5 \times MV \times C \times (\Delta YTM)^2]$$

For the eurobond in our example, the change in price due to convexity in dollars given a 150bp change in yield would be:

$$\Delta Price(\$)_{CONV} = [.5 \times 58.07 \times 1,000 \times (.0150)2] = \$6.53$$

The total price change of a bond in response to a change in rates is equal to the sum of the impact of the 1st derivative function (duration) and the 2nd derivative function (convexity).

$$\Delta Price(\$)_{TOTAL} = \Delta Price(\$)_{DUR} + \Delta Price(\$)_{CONV}$$

Again using the 10-year 10% eurobond, calculate the change in price due to 100bp change in rates. If rates rise, the change in price due to duration and convexity is:

$$\Delta MV_{DUR} = MV \times MD \times \Delta YTM$$
$$\Delta MV_{DUR} = \$1,000 \times -6.15 \times .0100 = -\$61.50$$

$$\Delta MV_{CONV} = .5 \times MV \times C \times (\Delta YTM)^2$$
$$\Delta MV_{CONV} = .5 \times 1{,}000 \times 58.07 \times (.0100)^2 = \$2.90$$
$$\Delta Price(\$)_{TOTAL} = -\$61.50 + \$2.90 = -\$58.60$$

If rates decline, the total price change would be:

$$\Delta MV_{DUR} = \$1{,}000 \times -6.15 \times -.0100 = \$61.50$$
$$\Delta MV_{CONV} = .5 \times 1{,}000 \times 58.07 \times (-.0100)2 = \$2.90$$
$$\Delta Price(\$)_{TOTAL} = \$61.50 + \$2.90 = \$64.40$$

Thus, given a symmetric 100bp change in yields, an investor would profit by \$64.40, but only lose \$58.60. Since the projected gain exceeds the loss, price convexity benefits the investor.

As another example, calculate the impact of a 100bp change in rates on a 30-year 8% ZCB that pays semiannually.

First calculate the MD. For this bond:

$$MD = \frac{Duration}{1 + \dfrac{YTM}{PPY}} + \frac{60}{1 + \dfrac{.08}{2}} = 57.69 / 2 = 28.85$$

Next, calculate the C. For this bond:

$$C = \frac{n \times (n+1) \times PVCFn}{PVCFn \times PPY^{PPY}} \times \frac{1}{\left[1 + \dfrac{YTM}{2} \right]^2}$$

$$C = \frac{60 \times 61 \times \$95.06}{\$95.06 \times 2^2} \times \frac{1}{\left[1 + \dfrac{.08}{2} \right]^2} = 847.97$$

Then calculate the total change in price if interest rates rise and fall by 100 basis points. If rates fall:

$$\Delta \text{Price}(\$)_{\text{DUR}} = \$95.06 \times 28.85 \times (-.0100) = \$27.42$$
$$\Delta \text{Price}(\$)_{\text{CONV}} = .5 \times \$95.06 \times 845.97 \times (-.0100)^2 = \$4.02$$
$$\Delta \text{Price}(\$)_{\text{TOTAL}} = +\$31.44$$

If rates rise:

$$\Delta \text{Price}(\$)_{\text{DUR}} = \$95.06 \times 28.85 \times (-.0100) = -\$27.42$$
$$\Delta \text{Price}(\$)_{\text{CONV}} = .5 \times \$95.06 \times 845.97 \times (-.0100)^2 = \$4.02$$
$$\Delta \text{Price}(\$)_{\text{TOTAL}} = -\$23.40$$

The Factors That Impact Convexity

Three basic rules explain how a bond's characteristics impact its price convexity and how to estimate the relative convexities of different bonds.

- If yield and maturity are held constant, as a bond's coupon declines its convexity increases.
- If yield and modified duration are held constant, as a bond's coupon declines, its convexity decreases.
- As maturity increases arithmetically, convexity generally increases exponentially.

Constant Yield and Maturity

If yield and maturity are held constant, as a bond's coupon declines its convexity increases. Thus, the convexity of a 5-year ZCB priced to offer an 8% YTM will be greater than the convexity of any 5-year coupon bond priced to offer the same return. The lower the coupon, the higher the convexity.

PROBLEM 12A

Calculate the price of 30-year euro zero offering yields from 2% to 20%. Graph the result. What is the price of the bond if it offers a 10% return? Suppose an investor thought there was a 50% chance rates would rise by 1% and a 50% chance rates would fall by 1%. What would the bond be worth then?

ANSWER:

Figure 12.5 presents the graphed result of the price calculation of the euro ZCB.

FIGURE 12.5

Zero Coupon Bond Chart Showing Convexity and Pricing Table

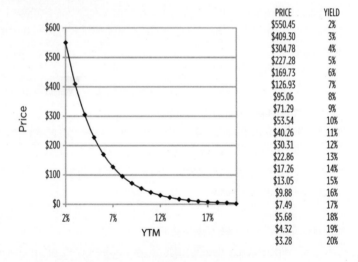

PRICE	YIELD
$550.45	2%
$409.30	3%
$304.78	4%
$227.28	5%
$169.73	6%
$126.93	7%
$95.06	8%
$71.29	9%
$53.54	10%
$40.26	11%
$30.31	12%
$22.86	13%
$17.26	14%
$13.05	15%
$9.88	16%
$7.49	17%
$5.68	18%
$4.32	19%
$3.28	20%

At a 10% return, the bond is worth $53.54.

A 50/50 of the 11% and 9% price is ($71.29 + 40.46) / 2
= $55.77.

The bond is worth more when volatility is expected.

Constant Yield and Modified Duration

If yield and modified duration are held constant, as a bond's coupon declines, its convexity decreases. Thus, the convexity of a 5-year ZCB priced to offer 8% will be lower than the convexity of any other bond with same MD. In order for another bond to have the same MD, it would, of course, have to have a longer life. The wider the dispersion of cash flows, the higher the convexity.

Constant Yield and Coupon

As maturity increases arithmetically, convexity generally increases exponentially. This leads to one of the most common trades: the bullet barbell trade. Consider the graph presented in Figure 12.6. It shows 3 ZCBs: a 2-year, a 4-year, and a 6-year. Since they are ZCBs, the maturities and durations are the same. Suppose you wanted to build a portfolio that had a duration of 4 years.

FIGURE 12.6

Yield vs. Maturity / Duration for ZCBs

There are three ways to do this without taking short positions:

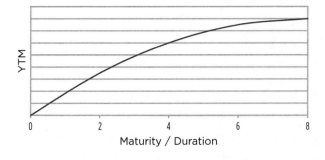

Implementing a Bullet vs. Barbell Trade

- Put 100% into the 4-year ZCB (known as the bullet)
- Put 50% into the 2-year and 50% into the 6-year (known as the barbell)
- Put a third into each (known as the ladder—but note is a combination of the bullet and barbell)

All have durations of 4 years, but which has the highest yield? Figure 12.7 shows the bullet and barbell.

FIGURE 12.7

Bullet vs. Barbell Play

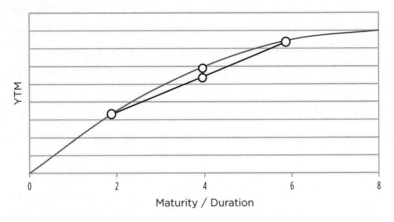

Because the graph shown in Figure 12.7 has some curvature, the bullet offers a higher yield than the barbell. Since the ladder is just the combination of the two, its yield is in between. If the bullet offers a higher return why would anyone want to buy the barbell? The answer is the barbell offers higher convexity and will outperform on a total return basis if interest rate volatility increases, as shown in Figure 12.8.

FIGURE 12.8

Bullet-Barbell Trade-Off

Portfolio	Yield	Convexity
Bullet	High	20
Ladder	Mod	20.67
Barbell	Low	24

The Higher Derivatives

As we stated earlier, modified duration is the 1st derivative of the price/yield function and convexity is the 2nd derivative of the price/yield function. There is also a 3rd derivative, a 4th derivative, a 5th derivative, and so on. You generally don't need to consider these because in the 3rd derivative the yield change is cubed, in the 4th derivative the yield change is raised to 4th power, and so forth. Thus, unless the interest rate change is very large, the impact of these functions on the price is minimal.

The only exception is when the size of the cash flows of the security themselves change as interest rates change. For example, the projected cash flows generated by interest-only collateralized mortgage obligations change dramatically as interest rates change. In this case, duration and convexity alone are not enough to describe the behavior of the security, and the higher derivative functions have to be used.

CHAPTER THIRTEEN

Credit Risk

When most people hear the term "credit risk," they interpret it as the risk that a payment they are owed will be missed, late, or only partially paid—in other words, a default will occur. Defaults are certainly instances of credit risk, but credit risk extends far beyond defaults. Investors can suffer losses on a note even when all the payments are made in full and on time. The losses in this case are indirect and result from the deterioration of credit quality. For example:

- Suppose a bank holds a large quantity of A rated bonds. They are later downgraded to BB+. Even though no payments have been missed the bank may have to hold a larger reserve against the bonds. This reduces the amount the bank can lend and thus reduces the bank's income.
- Suppose a fixed income mutual fund portfolio manager has purchased a large quantity of A rated bonds that are subsequently downgraded. As they are downgraded, their value declines, which causes the value of the fund's shares to de-

cline, which causes some current investors to sell and some potential investors to look elsewhere. The value of the fund's portfolio declines and, because the manager gets a fee based on the assets under management, the manager's fee declines— despite the fact that every cash flow has been received in full and on time.

- Suppose an insurance company owns some bonds that are downgraded from investment grade to high yield. Regulations may require the company to sell the bonds at a loss even if the company believes the bonds will not default. When the company reinvests the reduced sales proceeds, it will suffer a reduction of cash flow.
- Suppose you sold credit protection on $100MM of Ford Motor company bonds. The bond's credit quality declines causing the bond's value to decline to $80MM. Since you sold credit protection, you are marked to the market and must transfer $20MM to the bondholder even though there has been no default. Two years later, the bonds recover, and the $20MM is returned to you. Even though you eventually got your $20MM back, you still lost the interest you could have earned on that $20MM while it temporarily transferred to the protection buyer.

The bottom line is that credit risk is much broader than just default risk.

Working with credit as an investor distills down to two questions:

- What are you paid for assuming credit risk?
- What should you be paid for assuming credit risk?

It's very simple. If a bond is paying investors 200 basis points for assuming credit risk and 100 basis points is the fair compensation, the bond is a buy! However, if a bond is paying investors 75 basis points for credit risk but 100 basis points is fair compensation, the bond is a sell. Let's start with looking at how we determine what an investor is being paid for assuming credit risk.

The starting point of this analysis is the total spread. The total spread is the yield spread between the bond and the equivalent risk-free investment(s). For example, suppose a 10-year risk-free T-note yields 8%, and a 10-year risky investment yields 10%. The spread is 2% or 200 basis points.

The spread can be quoted to the US Treasury or the fixed side of an interest rate swap with the same maturity or the same duration. The spread can also be to the Treasury or the swap zero coupon curves.

Regardless of which you use as the base rate for defining the spread, many investors refer to the total spread as the credit spread. That is *not* correct. The total spread compensates the investor for at least eight other risks in addition to default risk. These risks include:

- Tax risk
- Tax increase risk
- Liquidity risk
- Cost of analysis risk
- Credit drift risk
- Credit convexity risk
- Uncertainty risk
- Embedded option risk

Only after subtracting the fair compensation for the other five risks from the total spread can we determine what the investor is receiving for credit risk. Let's look at each of these risks in turn.

Tax Risk

For an investor who is subject to taxes, the goal is to maximize the after-tax return. In the United States, the interest received from risk-free Treasuries is only subject to federal income tax, while the interest received from risky corporate bonds is subject to federal, state, and city income taxes. Given tax rates of 35% federal, 6% state, and 4% city and assuming that federal taxes are deductible at the state level and both federal and state are deductible at the city level, the after-tax incomes are:

$$\text{Treasury} = 8\% \times (1 - .35) = 5.2\%$$
$$\text{Corporate} = 10\% \times (1 - .35) = 6.5\% \times (1 - .06)$$
$$= 6.11\% \times (1 - .04) = 5.87\%$$

Taxes reduce the spread for the remaining risks from 200 basis points to 67 basis points (5.87% to 5.2%). This is not the entire tax impact.

Tax Rate Increase

If, in the future, the state and/or city tax rates increase, the spread between the two returns would narrow even further. Investors considering investing in a risky asset must be sure that they receive adequate compensation—not just for the impact of taxes today, but also for the impact of potentially higher tax rate rates in the future. Also, if either bond is purchased at a discount, the differential between the income and capital gains tax rates will also impact the after-tax spread.

The important point is that since everyone's tax rates and assumptions regarding future tax rates are going to be different, so will everyone's after-tax credit spread. The spreads on Bloomberg, the WSJ, and the evening news usually assume zero taxes and are grossly incorrect for the vast majority of investors.

LIQUIDITY

The only advantage to the United States being more than $17 trillion in debt is that the US Treasury market is remarkably liquid. If a security is liquid, it can be bought or sold:

- Quickly
- At a fair price
- With no or minimal market impact

You can buy or sell $100MM in Treasuries immediately, at fair value, and not have your trade move the market—not so with most corporate bonds. While there are a few liquid corporate bonds (usually issued by America's largest companies), the vast majority of corporate bonds are significantly less liquid. This means the dealer's bid-ask spreads are wider to compensate. Also, when you buy or sell, you can end up competing against yourself because your transaction alone moves the market.

For example, you want to by $50MM of the 8% XYZs of Aug 15, 2032. The current best bid and offer is 102 by 103. As you buy the bonds—starting at 103—your buy causes the price to rise, so your order is completed as follows:

$10MM at 103
$10MM at 103⅛

$10MM at 103¼
$10MM at 103⅜
$10MM at 103½

Thus, your average price was 103¼. Now, however, the bid ask spread is 102½ by 103½, so the price has to rise by ¾ of a point just to break even.

Different investors place different value on liquidity. An investor who buys and holds to maturity is less interested in liquidity than a portfolio manager who actively trades. To price liquidity, each investor has to solve the following equation for his own circumstances:

Price of liquidity = Probability of sale
   × Estimated costs of selling

Thus, an investor who thought liquidity would cost 100 basis points but who also thought there was a 5% chance of sale would put the cost of liquidity at 5 basis points. This reduces the total spread by another 5 basis points.

COST OF ANALYSIS

Managing a portfolio of US Treasuries requires only macroeconomic research. How will the yield curve shift? What will the inflation rate be? What actions, if any, will the Fed take? Since the US government can print money, there's no need for microeconomic credit analysis. However, when managers add corporate bonds to their portfolios, they almost always incur additional expenses, including the cost of:

- Subscribing to Moody's and Standard & Poor's credit services
- Adding credit analysts (salaries, office space, technology, and the like)
- Upgrading their trustee relationship to allow for corporate events (takeovers, bond conversions, and the like)

All of these additional costs have to be paid from the spread because they are only necessary for owners/managers of corporate bonds. The impact on the spread will depend on the additional costs incurred as well as the size of the corporate bond portfolio. If these costs total $1MM a year and the portfolio is a $1 billion portfolio, then 10 basis points of the spread just pays for the cost of analysis.

CREDIT DRIFT RISK

If an investor with $100MM to invest was to select 100 Baa rated bonds, invest $1MM in each one, and hold them over time, some of the bonds would experience credit upgrades and some of the bonds would experience downgrades. Over time, however, the investor will experience more downgrades than upgrades. It doesn't matter if the economy is weak, normal, or strong; there are always more downgrades than upgrades. Figure 13.1 depicts the credit drift for industrial bonds over a 5-year period.

FIGURE 13.1

Credit Drift

CURRENT RATING		Rating in 5 Years							
		AAA	AA	A	BBB	BB	B	CCC	D
	AAA	89.5	5.9	1.1	0.6	0	0	0	0
	AA	0.2	90.3	7.0	2.5	0	0	0	0
	A	0	3.6	86.4	8.3	1.7	0	0	0
	BBB	0	0.1	4.2	81.4	11.2	3.1	0	0
	BB	0	0	0.8	6.1	76.6	13.6	3.9	0
	B	0	0	0	1.2	7.8	54.2	32.5	4.3
	CCC	0	0	0	0	2.3	12.25	42.2	35.7
	D	0	0	0	0	0.1	1.2	5.3	31.4

Looking at the BBB bonds, only 81% still have a BBB bond rating after 5 years. The number of full downgrades to BB is almost three times the number of full upgrades to A. The number of double downgrades is more than 30 times the number of double upgrades.

The reason why there are more downgrades than upgrades is that once a company borrows the money it needs, management doesn't care about the bondholders. Management is elected by the shareholders, and management's number one goal is to reward shareholders. Many of the actions that management takes to reward shareholders can penalize bondholders, including raising dividends and buying back shares.

CREDIT CONVEXITY RISK

Even if an investor was so good at selecting bonds that the portfolio experienced the same number of upgrades and downgrades, the value of a portfolio will still decline over time. The reason for this is that a bond's price declines more on a downgrade than it rises on an upgrade. There is a larger change in yield in a downgrade than an upgrade. In Figure 13.2, the baseline is the yield of the US Treasury. As the credit quality declines, the incremental spreads increase by an ever-increasing amount.

FIGURE 13.2

Credit Convexity

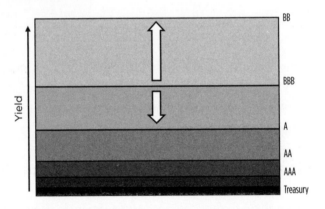

UNCERTAINTY PREMIUM

The cost of credit default risk is equal to the:

Amount at risk × the probability of default
× the percentage lost in default

At least two of those variables can only be estimated. This introduces a source of uncertainty in the arbitrage relationship between risk-free and risky investments. Suppose that a risk-free bond portfolio yields 8% and that a risky portfolio of corporates is expected to yield 8% after all defaults and delays. Because the corporate bond return can only be estimated, many managers demand that the expected return of the corporate portfolio exceed the return from the risk-free portfolio before they consider it to be equal. Thus, a manager might require that the expected return on the corporate portfolio exceed the risk-free portfolio by 10 basis points before considering them to be "equally" attractive. Each manager and investor sets their own uncertainty spread.

EMBEDDED OPTIONS

If a bond is callable, the investor has sold the issuer the right to redeem the bond early. The issuer will call the bond if rates decline and the company can issue new debt at a lower rate. Of course, this forces the investor to reinvest at a lower rate—lowering the investor's RCY, NRCY, or NNRCY. The premium the investor receives for selling this option is incorporated into a higher spread. To illustrate this process, we'll look at two embedded option pricing models: an admittedly oversimplified model that just illustrates the concept and the Bloomberg Single Factor Option-Adjusted Spread (OAS) Model.

Simplified Embedded Option Pricing Model

In this model, we're going to build a price tree and use that tree to value the bond under the assumption that there are no options. Then, we're going to adjust the price tree for an option and value the bond again. When we add an option to the tree, we will get a lower value for the bond. Since the only change we made was to add the impact of an option, the difference in the values must equal the value of the option. To illustrate, let's start with a note that is currently selling at $1,010 and is callable for the next 4 months at a price of $1,020. To keep the model simple, we'll build a binomial tree. Since the note has experienced an average price change of $10 per month and there is a 50/50 chance that interest rates will increase or decrease each month, the tree would be as shown in Figure 13.3.

FIGURE 13.3
Binomial Tree

								$1,050
							6.25%	6.25%
						$1,040		
					12.5%	12.5%	6.25%	
				$1,030				$1,030
			25%	25%	12.5%		18.75%	25%
		$1,020				$1,020		
	50%	50%	25%		25%	37.5%	18.75%	
$1,010				$1,010				$1,010
100%	50%		25%	50%	25%		18.75%	37.5%
		$1,000				$1,000		
		50%	25%		12.5%	37.5%	18.75%	
				$900				$900
				25%	12.5%		6.25%	25%
						$800		
					12.5%	6.25%		
								$700
								6.25%

Now, if starting at $1,010, we flip a coin, it comes up heads, and the price goes up. We flip again, it comes up tails, and the price goes down. We continue flipping with the results being noted in the path through the tree shown in Figure 13.4. Since we don't know where along this path the investor will sell the bond, we calculate the average price along the path. Clearly the average price along this path is $1,010. Some of the paths would have higher average prices. Some paths would have lower average prices. But, if you ran thousands of random paths through this tree, the average of the averages would be very close to $1,010.

FIGURE 13.4
Random Path from Tree

Now, let's add the call option that allows the issuer to call the bond at $1,020. Adding this option effectively caps the note at $1,020. (Even if the bond is not called, the fact that the bond can be called at $1,020 will prevent anyone from paying more than $1,020 for the bond.) This reduces the average price along the paths along the top of the tree (as shown in Figure 13.5) and the amount the investor can expect from investing in this bond. The average price along the paths drops to $1,008.375 from $1,010.00.

FIGURE 13.5

Lower All Values Higher Than $1,020

Adding the option reduces the investor's expected return by $1.625, so if the option is added the investor needs to either receive $1.625 upfront—or a higher yield that has a present value of $1.625. If 12 basis points per year had a present value of $1.625, then 12 basis points of the spread would just pay the investor for the option the investor sold to the issuer. Figure 13.6 shows the paths after adding the call option.

FIGURE 13.6

Paths After Adding Option

Path	Value 1	Value 2	Value 3	Value 4	Value 5	Average
1	$1,010	$1,020	$1,020	$1,020	$1,020	$1,018
2	$1,010	$1,020	$1,020	$1,020	$1,020	$1,018
3	$1,010	$1,020	$1,020	$1,020	$1,020	$1,018
4	$1,010	$1,020	$1,010	$1,020	$1,020	$1,016
5	$1,010	$1,020	$1,010	$1,020	$1,020	$1,012
6	$1,010	$1,020	$1,020	$1,020	$1,010	$1,016
7	$1,010	$1,020	$1,010	$1,020	$1,010	$1,014
8	$1,010	$1,020	$1,010	$1,000	$1,010	$1,010
9	$1,010	$1,000	$1,010	$1,020	$1,010	$1,010
10	$1,010	$1,000	$1,010	$1,000	$1,010	$1,006
11	$1,010	$1,000	$990	$1,000	$1,010	$1,002
12	$1,010	$1,020	$1,010	$1,000	$990	$1,006
13	$1,010	$1,000	$1,010	$1,000	$990	$1,002
14	$1,010	$1,000	$990	$1,000	$1,010	$1,002
15	$1,010	$1,000	$990	$980	$990	$994
16	$1,010	$1,000	$990	$980	$970	$990
				Average		$1,008.375
				Option Value		$1.625

So after allowing for the value of the other components of the spread, the actual spread for credit risk is 30 basis points—not 200 basis points, as depicted in Figure 13.7.

FIGURE 13.7

True Compensation for Default Risk After Cost of Other Risks Is Subtracted

	Cost of Risk	Treasury	Cost of Risk	Corporate	Spread
Nominal Yield		8.00%		10.00%	200
After Impact of Taxes	2.80%	5.20%	4.13%	5.87%	67
After Impact of Liquidity	0.00%	5.20%	0.05%	5.82%	62
After Additional Costs	0.00%	5.20%	0.05%	5.77%	57
Credit Drift	0.00%	5.20%	0.05%	5.72%	52
Credit Convexity	0.00%	5.20%	0.05%	5.67%	47
After Uncertainty	0.00%	5.20%	0.10%	5.62%	42
After Embedded Option	0.00%	5.20%	0.12%	5.50%	30

Thus, while the total spread is 200 basis points, the actual compensation for credit risk is just 30 basis points. This is the spread that should be used for relative value analysis. This answers the question "What are you getting paid for taking credit risk?"

BLOOMBERG OAS MODEL

The Bloomberg OAS model is used to estimate the value of embedded options. The model uses a binomial rate tree, as opposed to the price tree used in the simplified model we just reviewed. It is calibrated off the Interest Rate Swap curve instead of the US Treasury curve for two reasons:

- Treasuries are not priced at par. This causes a distortion in the creation of the spot curve and the forward curve. New swaps are priced at par which allows less distortive spot and forward curves to be derived.

- Interest rate swaps have less basis risk. In a political/economic crisis, there is often a flight to quality. This means Treasury yields decline while all other yields rise. Since embedded options are found in corporate bonds, which almost never have an AAA rating, their value should move with lower quality instruments—not Treasuries.

In this model, it is assumed that future interest rates are distributed around the forward swap curve, and that the width of the distributions is based solely on the current volatility of short-term rates. Because the width of the distribution is based solely on the current volatility of short-term rates, this model is often referred to as the "Bloomberg single factor model."

Building the Tree

From the current IRS swap rates, calculate the zero coupon swap rates. From the zero coupon rates, calculate the forward swap rates.

For example, if the spot swap rates are:

- 1-year swap = 7%
- 2-year swap = 7.4988%
- 3-year swap = 7.9969%

Then the forward interest rate swap rates, as shown in Figure 13.8, are:

- 1-year swap = 7%
- 1-year swap in 1 year = 8% = $\{[(1 + .074988)^2] / [1 + .07^1]\} - 1$

- 1-year swap in 2 years = 9% = {[(1 + .079968)^3] / [(1 + .074988)^2]} − 1

Once the forward rates are determined, the width of the distribution of possible rates around the 1-year rate in 1 year can be determined using the formulas shown in Figure 13.9 and Figure 13.10.

FIGURE 13.8

Possible Distribution of Rates

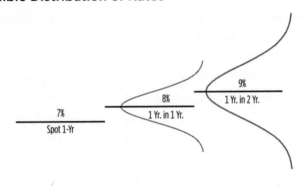

FIGURE 13.9

1-Year Rate in 1 Year, Formula 1

(Probability of rates declining × Weighted average of
  the lower rates) + (Probability of rates rising
  × Weighted average of the higher rates)

Normally, we assume a 50/50 chance of rates rising vs. falling.

FIGURE 13.10

1-Year Rate in 1 Year, Formula 2

Q = Weighted average (by probability) of rates above
the Implied Forward Rate / Weighted average (by
probability) of rates below the Implied Forward Rate

$Q = e^{2\sigma Sqrt(t)}$

Weighted average high rates = Q × Weighted average low
rates

If the volatility of short-term rates is 15%, then

$Q = e^{2(.15)sqrt(1)} = 1.35$

.5(weighted average of higher rates) + .5(weighted average
of lower rates) = 8%

This second equation has two variables, and thus it has an infinite number of solutions. However, we know the weighted average of higher rates is 1.35 times the weighted average of lower rates, thus this second equation (shown in Figure 13.11) becomes:

.5(1.35 × weighted average of lower rates) + .5(weighted
average of lower rates) = 8%

1.175 (weighted average of lower rates) = 8%

Low rate = 6.81%

High rate = 1.35 × 6.81 = 9.19%

Verify .5(9.19) + .5(6.81) = 8%

FIGURE 13.11

Building a Binomial Rate Tree for the Bloomberg Single Factor OAS Model

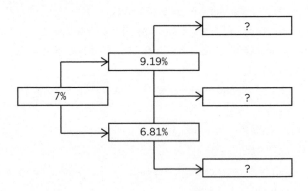

At the next (third) step of the tree, the probabilities and weighted average are:

.25(High rate) + .50(Middle rate) + .25(Low rate) = 9%
    (1-year rate in 2 years)

Restating the three variables in terms of one variable results in the following, which is shown graphically in Figure 13.12:

.25(1.35^2 Low rate) + .50(1.35 Low rate) + .25(Low rate)
   = 9%
1.38(Low rate) = 9%
Low rate = 6.52%
Middle rate = (6.52% × 1.35) = 8.8%
High rate = (8.8% × 1.35) = 11.88%

FIGURE 13.12

Restating the Three Variables in Terms of One Variable

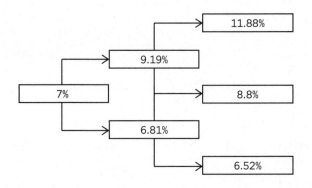

This process would be repeated, going out for up to 30 years. Once the tree is created it, can be used to:

- Value AA rated bullet bonds assuming a volatile rate environment
- Value AA rated bonds with embedded options
- Value bonds with other credit ratings

It is a very versatile and powerful tool as we shall see below, starting by using the tree to calculate the impact of volatility on price.

IMPACT OF VOLATILITY ON PRICE

A bond has a different value in a volatile as opposed to a nonvolatile interest rate environment. To illustrate, let's value a 9% 3-year eurobond. Let's first value it assuming zero volatility, in which case the bond is equal to the present value of its future cash flows as depicted in Figure 13.13.

FIGURE 13.13

Today	1 Year	2 Year	3 Year
	7%	8%	9%

$84.11	$90		
$77.88		$90	
$865.35			$1,090
$1,027.35			

Now, let's value the bond using the tree. There are four paths through this tree, each of which has a 25% of occurring. The bond's cash flows have to be present valued four different ways:

> If rates rise twice, then the value = $1,090 / (1.1188) / (1.0919) / (1.07) + $90 / (1.0919) / (1.07) + $90 / (1.07) = $995.03
>
> If rates rise then fall, then the value = $1,090 / (1.088) / (1.0919) / (1.07) + $90 / (1.0919) / (1.07) + $90 / (1.07) = $1,018.63
>
> If rates fall then rise, then the value = $1,090 / (1.088) / (1.0681) / (1.07) + $90 / (1.0681) / (1.07) + $90 / (1.07) = $1,039.47
>
> If rates fall twice, then the value = $1,090 / (1.0652) / (1.0681) / (1.07) + $90 / (1.0681) / (1.07) + $90 / (1.07) = $1,058.24
>
> Average = $1,027.84

When valued using the tree (incorporating volatility), this simple three cash flow note is worth an extra ($1,027.84 − $1,027.35) = $0.49. This is not the result of any rounding error. The reason for the discrepancy is that in a volatile environment, the price is expected to change and the bond's convexity (see Chapter 12) causes larger gains and smaller losses. Unless an investor expects interest rates to have no volatility, $1,027.84 is the more accurate valuation.

VALUING EMBEDDED OPTIONS

To value the embedded options, first work the cash flows back through the tree, as shown in Figure 13.14.

FIGURE 13.14
Value by Walking Back Through the Tree

					$1,090
				11.88%	
			$1,064.26		
		9.19%		11.88%	
	$1,077.30				$1,090
7%		9.19%		8.8%	
$1,027.84			$1,091.83		
7%		6.81%		8.8%	
	$1,122.27				$1,090
		6.81%		6.15%	
			$1,113.29		
				6.15%	
					$1,090

Sample calculation: {[.5 × ($1,090 / 1.1188)
+ .5 × ($1,090 / 1.1188)] + $90 payment} = $1,064.26

Thus, the price of the bond is $1,027.84. Now, suppose the bond is callable at par. In this case, every value above $1,090 has to be lowered to $1,090 as shown in Figure 13.15. This lowers the present value from $1,027.84 to $1,012.76, a difference of $15.08. The value of the option, therefore, is $15.08. This would have to be converted into a yield spread that had an equivalent PV.

FIGURE 13.15

Bond Callable at Par Alternative

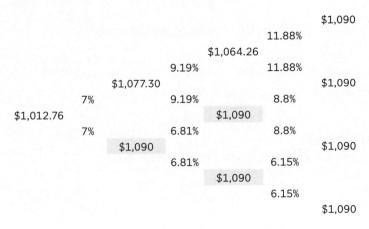

BONDS WITH DIFFERENT RATINGS

The original swaps that were used to create the yield tree were AA rated, and so the rates that result are appropriate only for AA rated bonds. If the bond has a different rating, a spread has to be added to each of the rates to account for the credit risk. Given the spread, the bond can be priced. If the bond already has a price, investors can work backwards to determine what spread needs to be added.

CHAPTER FOURTEEN

Pricing Credit Risk

What should you get paid for taking a credit risk? The answer can be determined from an arbitrage between risk free (US Treasuries) and risky (corporate bonds) assets. For example, if, after all credit defaults, delays, and expenses, a diversified portfolio of 10-year corporates *always* returned more than a 10-year Treasury, rational investors would always buy the diversified corporate bond portfolio. However, if the Treasury *always* yielded more, rational investors would only buy Treasuries. In order for investors to buy both corporates and Treasuries, half the investors have to be convinced that the corporate portfolio will outperform and the other half are convinced that the Treasuries will outperform, otherwise there is an arbitrage situation.

Of course, the level of credit risk in the corporate portfolio is always changing due to changing macro- and microeconomic factors. So, if the two portfolios offer the same net return today, but credit risk increases, the Treasury will be more attractive. If credit risk declines, the corporate portfolio will be more attractive. Naturally, investors often disagree about whether credit risk is increasing or decreasing—which makes a market a market.

PROBLEM 14A

Suppose a 5% 1-year AAA eurobond is priced at $1,000. If an investor thought a 1-year CCC rated eurobond had a 10% chance of default and, in the event of default, zero recovery, what would it have to yield to fairly compensate the investor for the credit risk, if it too was priced at $1,000?

ANSWER:

If the risk free investment grows $1,000 to $1,050 in a year, the risky investment has to do the same. Thus:

(The probability of default × default return)
   + (The probability of survival × survival return) = $,1050
(10% × $0) + (90% × $X) = $1,050
$1,050 / .9 = $1,166.67
Return = 16.67%

If the CCC rated note was yielding more than 16.67%, the investor should buy the corporate note—if it was yielding less, the investor should buy the risk-free alternative. If instead the recovery was 30%, the yield would have to be:

(10% × $300) + (90% × $X) = $1,050
$1,020 / .9 = $1,133.33
Return = 13.33%

PROBLEM 14B

Let's now look at a multiperiod example using a 3-year 10% eurobond priced at par. We assume default will only occur on an interest payment date since that's the only time the company has payments due. Suppose an investor thought the data depicted in Figure 14.1 would apply.

FIGURE 14.1

Determining Fair Compensation for Credit Risk Over Multiple Periods

Year	Projected Default Rate	Projected Loss	Fair Price	CPS	($)AR	Cost($)	Spot	PV
1	5%	50%	2.5%	100%	$1,100	$27.50	4%	$26.44
2	10%	60%	6%	95%	$1,045	$62.7	5%	$56.87
3	20%	70%	14%	85.5%	$973.5	$131.67	6%	$110.55
					Value of Credit Risk			$193.86

The fair price of credit risk is determined by multiplying the projected default rate by the projected loss in the event of default (Column 2 × Column 3). The conditional probability of survival (CPS) is the probability that the bond will still exist (that is, will not have defaulted) on the interest payment date, with the following:

- There is 100% probability the bond will make it to year 1 payment date.
- There is only a 95% probability the bond will make it to year 2 payment date. There is a 5% chance bond defaulted in year 1, so there is only a 95% chance the investor will need compensation for credit risk in year 2.
- There is only an 85.5% probability the bond will make it to year 3 interest payment date. There is 10% of a 95% chance (9.5%) the bond will default in year 2, so there is only an 85.5% chance the investor will need compensation for credit risk in year 3.

The annual amount at risk (($)AR) is ($1,000 principal + $100 interest) × CPS, which allows for previous defaults. The cost of credit protection paid on the interest payment date is determined by multiplying fair price by the annual amount at risk (Column 4 × Column 6). The spot rate from today to the interest payment date is shown in Column 8, and the PV of the cost of annual credit protection is shown in Column 9.

ANSWER:

The sum of Column 9 ($193.86) is the cost of buying a 3-year option that would protect the investor against default risk for 3 years. In the event of default:

- The investor would receive $1,100.
- The option seller would receive the note and would work through the bankruptcy process to recoup as much as possible.

Very often, protection buyers would rather pay for protection over time in a series of equal payments. Also, upon default, they want the payments to stop. In this case, we need to work backwards to determine the correct annual premium. The three premiums, when multiplied by the CPS and then discounted at the spot rates must total to $193.86—the cost of the option. Figure 14.2 illustrates the process.

FIGURE 14.2

Determining the Annual Credit Spread

Premium	CPS	Discount	Factor	CPS X Factor
X	100%	4%	.9615	.96150
X	95%	5%	.9070	.86165

Premium	CPS	Discount	Factor	CPS X Factor
X	85.5%	6%	.8396	.71786
		$193.86	/	2.5410
X =				$76.29

Determining Probability of Default from Credit Spread

If we can use the probability of default and percentage recovery to determine the correct spread, we should also be able to work backwards in order to determine the implied probability of default from the expected recovery and the spread.

If we accept the arbitrage relationship between Treasuries and corporates, invest $1 in Treasuries for 1 year (assuming continuous compounding and ignoring recovery), then the FV of that $1 invested in Treasuries can be determined using the following formula:

$$FV = PVe^{rt} = \$1PVe^{r1} = \text{which simplifies to: } e^r$$

The FV of that same $1 invested in corporates for 1 year (again, assuming continuous compounding) can be determined using the following formula, where:

- D = Default probability (you only get paid when bond *doesn't* default)
- s = Spread to Treasuries
- R = Recovery percentage

For $1 and 1 year this simplifies to:
$$FV = (1-D)e^{(r+s)}$$

Thus, the arbitrage between Treasuries and Corporates is:

$$e^{rt} = (1-D)e^{(r+s)t}$$

Rearranging the above gives us $D = 1 - e^{-st}$

Thus, if the spread is 100 basis points on a 1-year instrument, then:

$$D = 1 - e^{-.0100(1)} = .995\% \text{ or just under } 1\%$$

If we add a recovery, then the FV of the Corporate Bond would be:

$$FV = (1-D)PVe^{(r+s)t} + D(R)\, e^{(r+s)t}$$

This changes the probability of default to:

$$D = (1 - e^{-st}) / (1 - R)$$

PROBLEM 14C

Use the information and formulas just presented and confirm the data found in Figure 14.3.

FIGURE 14.3

Confirm These Values

Year	Treasury Spot Rates	BB Spot Rates	Credit Spread	Assumed Recovery	Implied Cumulative Probability of Default
1	3.00%	5.11%	2.11%	25%	2.78%
2	3.25%	5.79%	2.54%	25%	6.60%
3	3.45%	6.44%	2.99%	25%	11.44%
4	3.60%	6.93%	3.33%	25%	16.63%
5	3.70%	7.35%	3.65%	25%	22.24%
6	3.80%	7.66%	3.86%	25%	27.56%
7	3.95%	7.94%	3.99%	25%	32.49%
8	4.00%	8.10%	4.10%	25%	37.28%

Year	Treasury Spot Rates	BB Spot Rates	Credit Spread	Assumed Recovery	Implied Cumulative Probability of Default
9	4.04%	8.19%	4.15%	25%	41.56%
10	4.07%	8.27%	4.20%	25%	45.73%

BANKRUPTCY AND BONDS

Despite the best efforts of management teams, sometimes companies can't meet their current obligations and go bankrupt. The question then becomes, "What is a company that can't meet its obligations worth?" The process for valuing a bankrupt company has two steps. Step one is to determine if, despite failing to meets its obligations, the company is a viable company. A viable company is defined as one whose "black box" generates positive cash flow. The black box is described in Figure 14.4.

FIGURE 14.4

Company's Basic Black Box

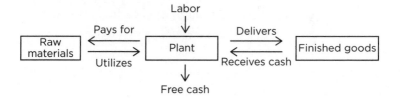

A company buys raw materials, applies labor at its plant to create finished goods, sells the finished goods for cash, uses the cash to pay for the raw materials and labor, and hopefully has free cash left over. If it does, it may be a viable business. If the company doesn't generate free cash, the business isn't viable and will be liquidated.

Some businesses' black boxes do generate significant free cash, but the free cash they generate is insufficient to cover one or more of the following:

- Service all the company's debt obligations.
- Meet their promised employee benefit obligations (health care and/or pension obligations).
- Pay any and all legal judgments and liabilities.

This suggests that if those liabilities could be reduced, these companies and the jobs they offer could be saved. This is the role of the bankruptcy court judge. The court determines:

- First, if the company is viable.
- Second, if the company is viable, which liabilities need to be postponed, reduced, or canceled in order to allow the company to return to profitability.

To do this, the court must first value the company. The value of the company will be equal to a multiple of the free cash the company generates less the mandatory capital expenditures (CapX).

- The free cash approximately is what drops down from the black box.
- The CapX are the mandatory capital expenditures (such as replacing worn-out equipment) the company must make just to keep operating at its current level. Note that these CapX expenditures are not designed to grow the company either horizontally or vertically.

- The mandatory CapX are subtracted from the free cash.
- The multiple applied to the remaining free cash flow is a function of the rate at which free cash is growing (or shrinking) and how damaged the business is by its having to file for bankruptcy. Figure 14.5 provides the approximate multiple for companies in bankruptcy.

FIGURE 14.5

Approximate Multipliers of (Free Cash – CapX) for Companies in Bankruptcy

Damage	Growth Rate of Cash Flows				
	0%	2%	4%	6%	8%
10%	9.1	10.6	12.6	15.1	18.4
12%	7.8	9.0	10.5	12.4	14.9
15%	6.5	7.3	8.3	9.7	11.3
18%	5.5	6.1	6.8	7.8	8.9
20%	4.9	**5.5**	6.1	6.8	7.7
25%	4.0	4.3	4.7	5.2	5.7
30%	3.3	3.6	3.8	4.1	4.5

Let's look at an example.

PROBLEM 14D

Suppose a company has free cash flow of $250MM and has $30MM of mandatory capital expenses it must make to keep operating. Based on the company's current condition and the rate at which its cash flow is growing, the multiple the judge uses is 6 times.

ANSWER:

The company is valued at:

$$6 \times (250\text{MM} - \$30\text{MM}) = \$1,320\text{MM}$$

With the value determined, we now turn to the company's capital structure, which is illustrated Figure 14.6.

FIGURE 14.6

Example Company Capital Structure

Debt	Amount
Bank debt	$220MM
Senior unsecured debt	$600MM
Subordinated debt	$750MM
Junior subordinated debt	$250MM

The total debt load is $1,820MM, and the company is only worth $1,320MM. In other words, it currently has -$500MM of equity. Clearly, this is untenable. In this circumstance, the judge might elect to cancel both the subordinate debt and the junior subordinate debt. By canceling $1,000MM in debt, the company goes from having -$500MM of equity to having +$500MM of equity, as shown in Figure 14.7.

FIGURE 14.7

Debt Load Following Subordinate and Junior Subordinate Debt Cancellation

Debt	Amount
Bank debt	$220MM
Senior unsecured debt	$600MM

Debt	Amount
Subordinated debt	$0MM
Junior subordinated debt	$0MM

The $500MM of equity will be given to the subordinated debt holders, since they have the senior claim relative to the junior subordinated debt. So the new capital structure will be as shown in Figure 14.8.

FIGURE 14.8

Example Company New Capital Structure Following Equity Distribution

Debt	Amount
Bank debt	$220MM
Senior unsecured debt	$600MM
Equity	$500MM

In the bankruptcy, the:

- Bank debt is left on the company's balance sheet.
- Senior unsecured debt is left on the company's balance sheet.
- The subordinated debt holders lose $750MM of debt but receive $500MM of equity. In short, they get $2 of equity for every $3 of debt they owned—a 66% recovery.
- The junior subordinated debt holders receive no equity because there isn't enough equity to make the debt level above them whole. They are wiped out, as are any lower levels in the capital structure.

Now, the interesting story of the above is the subordinated debt holders. As the company's credit quality declines, the value of the subordinated debt declines. The original purchasers (banks, insurance companies, individuals) sell in order to limit their loss. The buyers of this deeply distressed debt are the private equity and hedge funds. Let's suppose these secondary market buyers paid, on average, $0.50 on the $1 for the subordinated debt. Thus, the $750MM of subordinated debt cost them just $375MM.

In the bankruptcy, they exchange their bonds for $500MM worth of stock. So, they end up with 100% of the stock worth $500MM by losing bonds they bought for just $375MM—making $125MM in the bankruptcy process. They will hire a new management team to fix the company and grow it for a few years. Then, they will sell the company to a larger firm at a profit or take the company public. Every private equity manager will tell you that the best place to buy stock is not the floor of the New York Stock Exchange—but on the steps of the bankruptcy court.

When the various stakeholders agree on the value of the company and who should get what, they can go to the bankruptcy court with a prepackaged bankruptcy. In the example bankruptcy we just discussed:

- The bank is made whole, so it has no complaints.
- The senior bondholders are made whole with debt, so they have no complaints.
- The "current" subordinated debt holders made $125MM and ended up with 100% of the equity, so they are happy.
- The junior subordinated bondholders are unhappy but, even if the company was valued $150MM higher, they still wouldn't be entitled to any recovery.

CHAPTER FIFTEEN

Passive Fixed Income Portfolio Management

The term passive means one of two things; the investors want to:

- Tie the market's performance—and not try an outperform it. (Trying to outperform the market always entails the risk of underperforming the market.) The two most common ways to try to tie the market are through:
  - Ladder portfolios
  - Index matching
- Fund a liability or series of liabilities at the lowest cost possible. The three most common ways to fund specific liabilities are:
  - Zero coupon portfolios
  - Immunized portfolios
  - Dedicated portfolios

Let's look at how each is constructed, its advantages, disadvantages, and any special issues.

TIE THE MARKET: LADDER PORTFOLIOS

In a ladder portfolio, equal quantities of bonds are purchased that mature at set intervals along the yield curve. For example, a ladder could have $20K worth of bonds that mature each December for the next 15 years. Each year when the bonds mature, the principal is reinvested in a new 15-year bond. In effect, the portfolio is an endless conveyor belt. The variables in a ladder portfolio include:

- **Length**—Does the ladder go out 10, 15, 30 years? This is simply a matter of investor preference.
- **Rung spacing**—Do bonds mature every 6 months, 12 months, 2 years, some other interval? The more frequently they mature, the more closely the return will track the market. However, buying bonds in larger lots is usually less expensive, so there is a cost trade-off.
- **Credit quality**—Ladder portfolios usually are built with very high-quality bonds so that credit isn't an issue. Any significant credit loss will distort the portfolio's results from the markets.

The advantages of this approach include:

- It is simple to implement.
- It is very low cost because it only requires buying and holding.
- Return will equal the market return (less costs) over the long term.

The disadvantages of this approach are that it is strictly regimented. Does it really make sense to roll over maturing debt into new 30-year bonds if interest rates are at all-time lows? Probably not, but this approach offers no flexibility.

TIE THE MARKET: MIRROR INDEX

Another way to tie the market is mirror a fixed income index. The most popular index is the Barclays Capital US Aggregate Bond Index (formerly known as the Lehman Aggregate). The index is composed of more than 8,700 bond issuers, including:

- US Treasuries
- US agencies
- Insured mortgage backed
- Foreign governments issued in the United States
- Investment grade liquid corporates

Mirroring an index used to be very difficult. Today, however, any investor can mirror an index with as little as $500. This became possible with the advent of exchange-traded funds that mirror the index. Here are some examples:

BND	Vanguard Total Bond Market ETF
AGG	iShares Core Total US Bond Market ETF
LAG	SPDR Lehman Aggregate Bond ETF
SCHZ	Schwab US Aggregate Bond ETF

Fund Liabilities: Zero Coupon Bonds

Regardless of whether an investor is looking to fund one liability or a large series of liabilities, one way to fund them is by funding each liability with a zero coupon bond that matures on the day the liability is due (or shortly thereafter). Because the bonds are ZCBs and the principal is spent as soon as it comes in, there is no reinvestment risk. Provided the bonds have a high credit quality, the position has little risk. The cost of funding the liabilities is known. The cash flows offset each other, and so the duration of the assets equals the duration of the liabilities.

Fund Liabilities: Dedicated Portfolio

A dedicated portfolio is another way to fund a set of liabilities. In a dedicated portfolio, you start by funding the longest liability with the *last payment* of a long-term coupon bond—not a zero coupon bond. In each of the earlier years, the bond's coupon payments are used to partially pay an earlier liability. Thus, when the bond's 1-year coupon is paid, it is immediately used to pay a part of a 1-year liability. When the 2-year coupon is paid, it is immediately used to pay part of a 2-year liability. When the 3-year coupon is paid . . .

By using this methodology, short-term liabilities are partially funded with long-term higher yielding assets. Then, the remaining balance of the next to longest liability is funded, and its coupons also reduce the earlier liabilities. Then, the next liability is funded until all the liabilities are funded.

An example will help illustrate.

PROBLEM 15A

Suppose a business owner buys out his partner and agrees to pay him $1MM a year for 20 years. The business owner wants to buy a portfolio that will fund the liabilities. The current yield on euro-bonds is as depicted in Figure 15.1.

FIGURE 15.1

New Issue Eurobond Yields

Current New Issue Eurobonds at Par							
Year	Rate	Year	Rate	Year	Rate	Year	Rate
1	3.00%	6	5.95%	11	6.73%	16	6.92%
2	4.00%	7	6.20%	12	6.79%	17	6.93%
3	4.75%	8	6.40%	13	6.84%	18	6.94%
4	5.25%	9	6.55%	14	6.88%	19	6.95%
5	5.65%	10	6.65%	15	6.91%	20	6.95%

ANSWER:

As is usually the case, the long-term bonds yield more than the short-term bonds, so we want to use as many on longer-term bonds in funding as possible.

Figure 15.2 depicts the dedicated portfolio worksheet used to work through the requirements:

- The top row contains the year in which payment is due (only years 10 through 20 are shown)
- The next row is the coupon of the par eurobond with the same maturity
- The third row is the initial size of the liability each year—$1MM
- The fourth row is the number of 20-year bonds required to

FIGURE 15.2

Dedicated Portfolio Worksheet

10	11	12	13	14	15	16	17	18	19	20
6.65%	6.73%	6.79%	6.84%	6.88%	6.91%	6.92%	6.93%	6.94%	6.95%	6.95%
$1MM	$1MM	$1MM	$1MM	$1MM	$1MM	$1MM	$1MM	$1MM	$1MM	$1MM
										$935
$64,983	$64,983	$64,983	$64,983	$64,983	$64,983	$64,983	$64,983	$64,983	$64,983	$999,983
									$935,018	
									$874	
$60,743	$60,743	$60,743	$60,743	$60,743	$60,743	$60,743	$60,743	$60,743	$934,743	
								$874,275		
								$818		
$56,769	$56,769	$56,769	$56,769	$56,769	$56,769	$56,769	$56,769	$874,769		
							$817,505			
							$765			
$53,015	$53,015	$53,015	$53,015	$53,015	$53,015	$53,015	$818,015			
						$764,491				
						$715				
$49,478	$49,478	$49,478	$49,478	$49,478	$49,478	$764,478				
					$715,013					
					$669					
$46,228	$46,228	$46,228	$46,228	$46,228	$715,228					
				$668,785						
				$626						
$43,069	$43,069	$43,069	$43,069	$669,069						
			$625,716							
			$586							
$40,082	$40,082	$40,082	$626,082							
		$585,634								
		$548								
$37,209	$37,209	$585,209								
	$548,425									
	$514									
$34,592	$548,592									
$513,832										
$482										
$514,053										

pay off the 20-year liability—935 bonds. Note that the answer here is not 1,000 bonds because the bonds pay interest at maturity that can also be used to pay the liability.

($935,000 Principal + ($935,000 × .0695 × 360 / 360))
= $999,983

- The fifth row is the cash flow generated by the bond: $64,983 of interest generated each year and $999,983 in year 20.
- The sixth row is the remaining liability for year 19. The remaining liability is the original $1MM liability less the interest payment generated by the 20-year bond ($64,983), which equals $935,017.
- The seventh row is the number of 19-year bonds required to retire the remainder of 19-year liability.
- The eighth row is the annual cash flows generated by the 19-year bond.
- The ninth row is the remaining 18-year liability after the interest payments from the 20-year and the 19-year bond are used to reduce it.
- The tenth row is the number of 18-year bonds required to retire the balance of the year 18-liability.

This loop continues until the first (1-year) liability is paid off.

The main issues with the construction of a dedicated portfolio are:

- **Credit requirements**—In this strategy, all bonds are held to maturity and a single bond might provide cash flows for 30 different annual liabilities. Therefore, if any bond develops credit issues, replacing it can be quite expensive.

- **Embedded options**—Bonds with embedded options should be excluded so that they don't disturb the cash flow matches.
- **Maturity mismatches**—Allowable maturity mismatches include:
  - Bonds that mature shortly before the liability is due are not a problem—provided that a conservative rate of return on investing the proceeds is assumed until the liability is paid.
  - Bonds that mature shortly after the liability is due must either be sold just prior to maturity (taking a small amount of market risk) or require the investor to pay the liability with borrowed money—and then use the maturity proceeds to pay off the loan.

FUND LIABILITIES: IMMUNIZED PORTFOLIOS

An immunized portfolio is another passive approach to managing a portfolio. However, unlike the last two approaches, while the duration matches, the cash flows don't. Let's start by considering a single $10MM liability due in 10 years. As a single cash flow, the duration of the cash bond is also 10. For this example:

- Suppose 10-year bonds yield 3%
- Suppose 12-year bonds yield 3.5%
- Suppose 14-year bonds yield 4%

The easiest way to fund this liability would be with a 10-year ZCB. A 10-year ZCB has a duration of 10 years. The cash flows and durations are a match, so the funding approach works. It is, however, the most expensive way of financing the liability because the return is only 3%. Another way to fund the liability is to use longer-term, higher yielding bonds to fund the liabilities. Because the bonds will have maturities longer than 10 years, the coupons will have to be higher than 0 to keep the duration at 10. Figure 15.3 looks at three alternatives.

FIGURE 15.3

Three Alternatives for Funding a 10-Year Liability

Maturity	10 Years	12 Years	14 Years
Coupon	0.00%	3.50%	6.97%
Yield	3.00%	3.50%	4.00%
Frequency	1	1	1
Duration	10	10	10
Funding Cost	$7,440,939	$7,089,102	$6,755,406

Funding the liabilities with the 14-year coupon bonds is the least costly of the three alternatives, *but there is a catch*. To illustrate the catch, let's start by using the 10-year zero coupon bond as a funding vehicle. In this case, as of today the liability and the asset both have durations of 10 years, as shown in Figure 15.4.

FIGURE 15.4

Initial Duration of 10-Year ZCB and 10-Year Liability

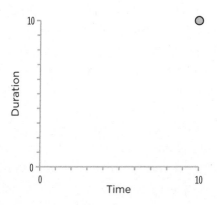

As time passes, the duration of the liabilities declines in a linear manner—that is, in 1 year, the liability has a duration of 9; in 2 years, 8; in 3 years, 7; and so on. Because the asset is a zero coupon bond, its duration also declines in a linear manner. Therefore, if the liability is funded with the 10-year zero, the durations not only start out equal—but stay equal over time, as shown in Figure 15.5.

FIGURE 15.5

Duration of 10-Year ZCB and Liability over Time

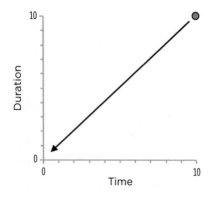

If instead, the liability is funded with the 14-year coupon bond, the durations start off equal but decline at different rates as time passes. After 10 years, the liability is due, but the bond would still have 4 years to maturity and a duration of approximately 3.5, depending on the yield. Clearly, while the durations start out equal, they decline at different rates, and the hedge breaks down, as shown in Figure 15.6.

FIGURE 15.6

Duration of Liability and Duration of 14-Year Bond over Time

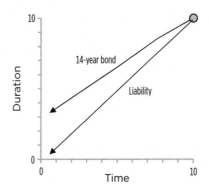

In order to use the 14-year bond as a hedge, it is necessary to periodically rebalance the hedge. This means shortening the duration of the asset so it equals the duration of the liability. There are two ways to shorten the duration: Periodically swap into lower-duration bonds or periodically add short T-note futures positions to the portfolio to lower the duration. Either will cost some money, but using the futures usually costs much less. Using the 14-year funding vehicle instead of the 10-year initially saved $685,533 ($7,440,939 − $6,755,406), as shown in Figure 15.7. If the costs of rebalancing the hedge plus the hedging error caused by a less than perfect hedge totals less than $685,533, it makes more sense to use the 14-year bond. If the costs are higher, use the 10-year.

FIGURE 15.7

Using the 14-Year Bond and Rebalancing

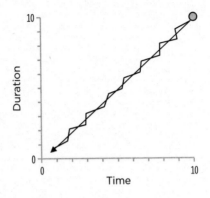

CHAPTER SIXTEEN

Active Portfolio Management

Investors who actively manage their portfolios try to outperform the market. They anticipate how the market will change and then position their portfolios to profit from that change. Active portfolio management usually requires additional trading, market data, analytics, and/or personnel, so the active strategy has to generate an extra return that exceeds these additional costs in order to provide real value added. Active strategies fall into two categories: Those that are designed to outperform an index and those that are designed to boost total return without regard to any index. Let's start with strategies that are designed to outperform an index.

For this section the index we will use is the Barclays Aggregate Taxable Index. This index includes US Treasuries, US agencies, investment grade corporates, and insured mortgage-backed securities. Let's assume it has the characteristics depicted in Figure 16.1.

FIGURE 16.1

Barclays Aggregate Data

Barclays Aggregate	
Weighted average coupon	4.96%
Weighted average maturity	12.22
Weighted average yield	3.96%
Duration	7.61
Modified duration	7.40
Convexity	21
Percent AAA	72%
Percent AA	16%
Percent A	5%
Percent BBB	7%
Percent Treasuries	31%
Percent agencies	14%
Percent corporates	19%
Percent mortgages	36%

There are three ways to outperform an index:

- Buy individual securities that mirror the index but are less liquid than the index.
- Buy four ETFs (Treasury, agency, MBS, corporates) held in percentages that mirror the index, and then make active reallocation bets.
- Buy three of the four ETFs, and actively manage the sector where the investor has a competitive advantage.

Let's look at these three alternative methodologies in greater detail.

LIQUIDITY APPROACH

Less liquid securities offer a higher yield than otherwise identical securities that are more liquid. An 8% A rated 20-year bond from a small offering will offer a higher yield than an 8% A rated bond from a $1 billion offering. A $1MM 6% GNMA with a $115K remaining balance will trade at a higher yield than a $1 billion 6% GNMA with an $800MM remaining balance. To the extent an investor can duplicate the index with less liquid securities, the investor can slightly outperform. However, this strategy makes sense only for long-term investors.

FOUR ETF APPROACH

An investor who buys four ETFs that collectively mirror the index can easily make volatility bets by overweighting/underweighting asset classes. Depending on expectations, the investor should use the following courses of action:

- **Interest rate volatility increases**—The investor should underweight the MBS ETF that has negative convexity and overweight the UST ETF that has positive convexity. Reverse the trade if interest rate volatility is expected to decline.
- **Credit spread declines**—The investor should overweight the CORP ETF and underweight the UST ETF. Reverse the trade if credit spreads are expected to widen.
- **Interest rate declines**—The investor should sell 5% or 10% of the ETF shares and buy long-term bonds, long-term zeros, and Treasury zeros. The long-term bonds have durations higher than 7.61 and so will boost the duration of the overall portfolio. If rates decline, the investor's portfolio will outper-

form. Stick with Treasuries to minimize transaction costs and maximize liquidity. After rates have declined, sell the Treasuries at a profit and repurchase shares in the ETF(s). Of course, if the investor expected rates to rise the investor should sell 5% to 10% of the ETF shares and invest in cash and/or floating rate notes that shorten the portfolio's duration relative to the index. If rates do rise, the investor's portfolio will suffer a smaller loss—and therefore outperform.

Three ETF Approach

In this approach, the investor buys three of the four ETFs—but actively manages the fourth market sector. For example, if the investor has a real expertise in credit analysis, the investor should buy the MBS, AGCY, and UST ETFs and actively manage the corporate bond portfolio. If the investor's skill allows them to outperform the corporate index and the investor ties the other three sectors, the portfolio as a whole will outperform.

Total Return

An investor who is not competing against a benchmark is said to be seeking total return. They can implement all of the strategies we just discussed, as well as a few strategies unique to total return investors. The two most common ones are:

- Riding the yield curve
- Yield curve plays

Let's look at them now.

Riding the Yield Curve

Suppose you want to invest $1MM for 1 year, and you have two choices:

- Bond A—Buy a 1-year $1,000 investment priced at par with a coupon of 5%.
- Bond B—Buy a 2-year $1,000 investment priced at par with a coupon of 6%, and sell it in a year.

If you expect the yield curve to remain unchanged over the next year, which is a better buy?

FIGURE 16.2
Initial Choice

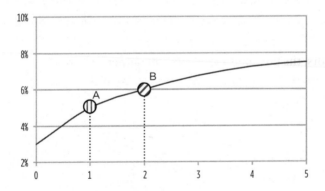

As shown in Figure 16-3, if the yield curve remains unchanged, then in 1 year:

- Bond A matures at par and yields 5%.
- Bond B still has a year of life left, and so must be sold. However, over the next year, the 2-year note becomes a 1-year

note. Thus, in 1 year, it's a 1-year note with a 6% coupon and could be sold at a premium.

FIGURE 16.3

After a Year

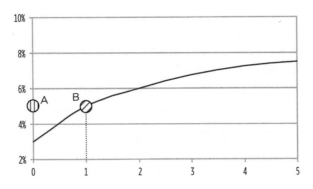

If the 6% coupon note is sold as a 1-year note offering a 5% return, the net performance of the two notes is as shown in Figure 16.4.

FIGURE 16.4

Relative Performance of Two Notes If Rates Stay Constant

	1-Year 5%	2-Year 6%
Buy	5%	6%
Sell	NA	5%
Income	$50	$60
Gain	$0	$9.52
Total	$50	$69.52

The 2-year note earns $69.52, instead of $50.00, which is an incremental return of $19.52 or 39%. Of course, buying the 2-year note and selling it in 1 year is not a risk-free strategy. If interest rates rise, the value of the 2-year note can decline. For example, suppose over the next year interest rates rise by 1%, as shown in Figure 16.5.

FIGURE 16.5
Interest Rates Rise by 1%

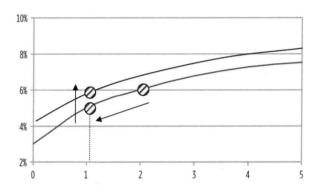

In this case, the benefit of riding down the yield curve from 2 years to 1 year is offset by the yield curve rising by 1%, as described in Figure 16.6.

FIGURE 16.6
Relative Performance of Two Notes If Rates Rise by 1%

	1-Year 5%	2-Year 6%
Buy	5%	6%
Sell	NA	6%
Income	$50	$60
Gain	$0	$0
Total	$50	$60

If rates rise by 1%, the 2-year note still generates an extra $10— or a 20% incremental return. One-year rates in 1 year would have to rise to almost 7% before the return on the two notes is equal and above 7% before the 1-year note offers a higher return.

The steeper the yield curve, the greater the advantage of riding down the curve. Look at the curves shown in Figure 16.7.

FIGURE 16.7

Two Curves

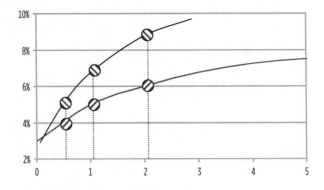

- Along the lower curve, as time passes the yield declines by 1% over the first year and another 1% over the next 6 months.
- Along the higher curve, as time passes the yield declines by 2% over the first year and another 2% over the next 6 months. The larger the decline in rates, the greater the rise in price.

Figure 16.8 provides details about the pricing of the coupon bonds along both curves.

FIGURE 16.8

Price of Current Coupon Bond Along Both Curves

	Start	In 1 Year	In 18 Months
High Curve	9%—$1,000	7%—$1,018.69	5%—$1,019.28
Low Curve	6%—$1,000	5%—$1,009.52	4%—$1,009.71

As time passes, there are two offsetting factors that impact the price of the note. The decline in rates causes the price to rise. The passage of time causes a pull toward par at maturity. If you hold the note too long, the pull toward par exceeds the benefit of rates declining. As a general rule, sell about halfway to maturity. If you buy a 2-year note when the yield curve is steep, sell it in a year. If you buy a 3-year note, sell it in 18 months. Reinvest the proceeds where the curve starts to be steep and reap the profits.

Making Yield Curve Bets

Yield curve shifts are often nonparallel. Short-term rates can be rising while long-term rates are stable—or even declining. Fed actions that have immediate impact at the short end of the curve may:

- Have no impact at the long-term rates
- Only have an impact after a lengthy delay
- Cause long-term rates to move the opposite way

Likewise, inflation can cause long-term rates to rise over a multi-year time frame before the Fed chooses to react by raising short-term rates. At the intermediate point of the curve, mortgage activity may heat up—putting pressure on the 10-year point of the curve, without materially impacting the short end or the long end of the curve. For example, suppose an investor expects the Fed to drastically raise short-term rates in an effort to control inflation and, as a result, you expect the yield curve to invert as illustrated in Figure 16.9.

FIGURE 16.9

Current vs. Expected Yield Curve

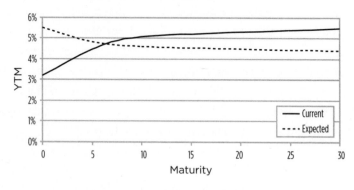

Given this outlook, you might want to go long 20-year euro ZCBs and short 1-year euro ZCBs. Assuming the 20-year ZCBs yields 6% and the 1-year ZCB yields 3%, the value of .01 ΔIR for each would be:

20-year = MV × MD × .0001
20-year = 1,000 / (1.06)^{20} × (20 / 1.06) × .0001
20-year = \$311.80 × 18.87 × .0001
20-year = \$0.588
1-year = MV × MD × .0001
1-year = 1,000 / 1.03^{1} × 1 / 1.03 × .0001
1-year = \$970.87 × .971 × .0001
1-year = \$0.0945

Thus, the ratio of bonds that is necessary to have equal volatility on both sides is 6.24. In this case, you would go short 6.24 1-year ZCBs for each long 20-year ZCB. By having equal volatility, the investor is not exposed to parallel shifts in rates. If rates rise or fall in general, the gain and loss offset each other. This position profits from a yield curve flattening and loses if the yield curve steepens. Assume an investor went short $6.4 MM of 1-year ZCBs and long $1MM of the 20-year ZCBs. If short rates rise 150 basis points and long rates decline 20, the net profit would be approximately:

Short position = 6,400 bonds × 50 × $.0945 = $30,200
Long position = 1,000 bonds × 20 × $.588 = $11,760

There are numerous opportunities to put on yield curve plays during the typical economic cycle, as shown in Figure 16.10.

FIGURE 16.10

Start of the Business Cycle

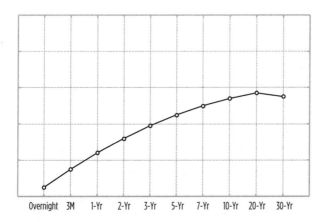

At the start of the business cycle, the yield curve normally has a positive slope, but it is fairly flat. As the economy heats up, inflation fears enter the economy, and long-term rates start to rise because long-term investors take more inflation risk, as depicted in Figure 16.11.

FIGURE 16.11

Long-Term Rates Rise

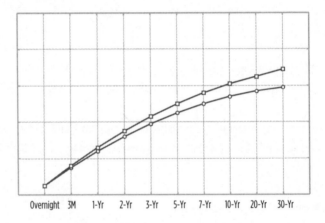

| Overnight | 3M | 1-Yr | 2-Yr | 3-Yr | 5-Yr | 7-Yr | 10-Yr | 20-Yr | 30-Yr |

When long-term rates start to rise, the Fed tends to react slowly, so long-term and short-term rates start to rise in conjunction with long-term rates. This rise is parallel, as shown in Figure 16.12.

FIGURE 16.12

Parallel Rise

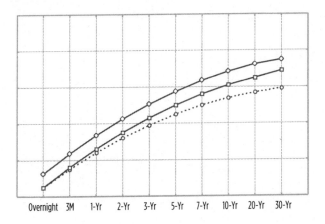

The Fed then gets serious about fighting inflation and raises short-term rates dramatically. This usually causes long-term rates to start declining, as shown in Figure 16.13.

FIGURE 16.13

Fed Dramatically Raises Short-Term Rates

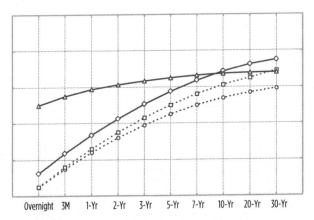

Sometimes the Fed overreacts and raises short-term rates too far, which results in an inverted yield curve. As a result, long-term rates fall faster, as illustrated in Figure 16.14.

FIGURE 16.14

Inverted Yield Curve

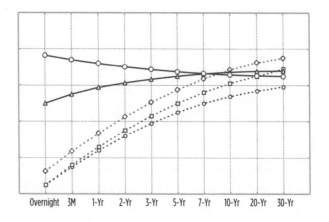

After successfully pushing down long-term rates, the Fed can lower short-term rates (Figure 16.15).

FIGURE 16.15

Fed Lowering Rates After Success

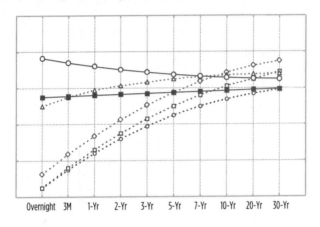

Overnight 3M   1-Yr   2-Yr   3-Yr   5-Yr   7-Yr   10-Yr   20-Yr   30-Yr

Then the cycle starts over, as illustrated in Figure 16.16.

FIGURE 16.16

The Cycle Repeats

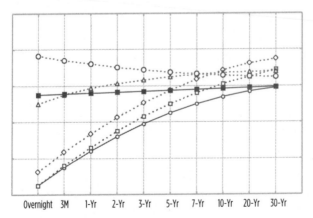

Overnight 3M   1-Yr   2-Yr   3-Yr   5-Yr   7-Yr   10-Yr   20-Yr   30-Yr

Some additional strategies that are beyond the scope of this text include:

- **More than one currency**—Global portfolios provide the opportunity to overweight bonds in currencies you expect to get stronger.
- **Covered option writing**—Selling out of the money options on bonds in the portfolio can allow you to generate additional revenue.
- **Future credit quality**—Predicting the future credit quality of individual bonds can also generate revenue.

Derivation of Modified Duration

The technical definition of modified duration is the first derivative of the price yield function. The term "derivative" means measures the change in. Modified duration measures the change in a bond's price in response to a change in interest rates. In mathematical notation, the function is sometimes expressed as depicted in Figure A.1.

FIGURE A.1

Modified Duration

$$\text{Modified Duration} = \frac{\Delta MV}{\Delta YTM}$$

While a math background makes understanding derivations a little easier, even those readers without a strong math background should be able to follow the step-by-step derivation offered next. (Understanding the derivation is not necessary for effectively using modified duration).

The market value of any series of future cash flows, such as the series of payments from a bond, is equal to the sum of the present value of the cash flows, where each cash flow is discounted by the periodic yield. The periodic yield, in turn, is equal to the YTM divided by the number of compounding periods per year, as described in the formula shown in Figure A.2.

FIGURE A.2
Periodic Yield Formula

$$\text{Market Value} = \frac{CF_1}{\left(1+\dfrac{YTM}{PPY}\right)^1} + \frac{CF_2}{\left(1+\dfrac{YTM}{PPY}\right)^2} + \cdots + \frac{CF_n}{\left(1+\dfrac{YTM}{PPY}\right)^n}$$

If we take the first derivative of the equation depicted in Figure A.2 with respect to the bond's yield, the resulting formula would be as shown in Figure A.3.

FIGURE A.3
First Derivative of the Periodic Yield Formula

$$\frac{\Delta MV\$}{\Delta YTM} = \frac{(-1)CF_1}{\left[1+\dfrac{YTM}{PPY}\right]^2} + \frac{(-2)CF_2}{\left[1+\dfrac{YTM}{PPY}\right]^3} + \cdots + \frac{-(n)CF_n}{\left[1+\dfrac{YTM}{PPY}\right]^{n+1}}$$

This equation, while correct, is overly complicated. To simplify the equation, factor out the quantity, as shown in Figure A.4.

FIGURE A.4

First Derivative of the Periodic Yield Formula Simplified to Factor Out Quantities

$$\frac{-1}{\left[1+\dfrac{YTM}{PPY}\right]}$$

When quantity is factored out of the right side of the equation, the result is as shown in Figure A.5.

FIGURE A.5

First Derivative of the Periodic Yield Formula Further Simplified

$$\frac{\Delta MV\$}{\Delta YTM}=\frac{-1}{\left[1+\dfrac{YTM}{PPY}\right]}\times\left[\frac{1\times CF_1}{\left[1+\dfrac{YTM}{PPY}\right]^1}+\frac{2\times CF_2}{\left[1+\dfrac{YTM}{PPY}\right]^2}+\cdots+\frac{n\times CF_n}{\left[1+\dfrac{YTM}{PPY}\right]^n}\right]$$

The elements of the equation within the large brackets can be restated in a more concise notation that results in the equation shown in Figure A.6.

FIGURE A.6

First Derivative of the Periodic Yield Formula More Concisely Notated

$$\frac{\Delta MV\$}{\Delta YTM}=\frac{-1}{\left[1+\dfrac{YTM}{PPY}\right]}\times\left[\sum_{1}^{n}\frac{n\times CF_n}{\left[1+\dfrac{YTM}{PPY}\right]^n}\right]$$

That last equation solves for the change in the market value of a bond (in dollars) for a small change in yield. If you divide the change in the market value (expressed in dollars) by the market value of the bond, the result gives you the change in the value of the bond expressed in percentage terms instead of dollar terms.

As shown in Figure A.7, to convert the change in price from dollar terms to percentage terms, multiply both sides of the equation by 1/MV—which is the same as dividing both sides by the MV.

FIGURE A.7

Converting the Change in Price from Dollar Terms to Percentage Terms

$$\frac{1}{MV} \times \frac{\Delta MV\$}{\Delta YTM} = \frac{1}{MV} \times \frac{-1}{\left[1 + \dfrac{YTM}{PPY}\right]} \times \left[\sum_{1}^{n} \frac{n \times CF_n}{\left[1 + \dfrac{YTM}{PPY}\right]^n}\right]$$

Which simplifies as shown in Figure A.8.

FIGURE A.8

Simplified Conversion from Dollar Terms to Percentage Terms

$$\frac{\Delta MV\%}{\Delta YTM} = \frac{-1}{\left[1 + \dfrac{YTM}{PPY}\right]} \times \frac{1}{MV} \times \left[\sum_{1}^{n} \frac{n \times CF_n}{\left[1 + \dfrac{YTM}{PPY}\right]^n}\right]$$

Further simplifying the equation within the brackets leads to the formula shown in Figure A.9.

FIGURE A.9

Further Simplified Conversion from Dollar Terms to Percentage Terms

$$\frac{\Delta MV\%}{\Delta YTM} = \frac{-1}{\left[1+\dfrac{YTM}{PPY}\right]} \times \frac{1}{MV} \times \left[\sum_{1}^{n} n \times PVCFn\right]$$

Multiplying the sum inside the parentheses by 1/MV yields the most common equation for expressing the change in price in percentage terms that results from a change in yield. The equation shown in Figure A.10 is known as the formula for modified duration.

FIGURE A.10

The Modified Duration Formula

$$\frac{\Delta MV\%}{\Delta YTM} = \frac{-1}{\left[1+\dfrac{YTM}{PPY}\right]} \times \frac{\displaystyle\sum_{1}^{n} n \times PVCFn}{MV}$$

Within the formula for modified duration, as shown in Figure A.11, is the formula for Macaulay's duration. Macaulay's duration is the last component of the equation.

FIGURE A.11

The Macaulay's Duration Formula

$$\text{Macaulay Duration in Periods} = \frac{\displaystyle\sum_{1}^{n} n \times PVCFn}{MV}$$

To calculate duration in years instead of in periods, divide the duration in periods by the number of payments per year (PPY). (See Figure A.12.)

FIGURE A.12

The Macaulay's Duration Expressed in Years

$$\text{Macaulay Duration in Years} = \frac{\sum_{1}^{n} n \times \text{PVCFn}}{\text{MV} \times \text{PPY}}$$

While modified duration measures the change in a bond's price (in percent) in response to a change in the bond's yield, Macaulay's duration measures the point along the bond's life where the $T\$R_{ACT}$ equals the $T\$R_{EXP}$. Thus, modified duration and Macaulay's duration are not synonymous, as shown in Figure A.13. Note that the terms are, unfortunately and incorrectly, often used interchangeably.

FIGURE A.13

The Relationship Between Modified Duration and Macaulay's Duration

$$\text{Modified Duration} = \frac{\Delta \text{MV}\%}{\Delta \text{YTM}} = \frac{-1}{(1+\text{YTM})} \times \text{Macaulay Duration}$$

Duration Program for an HP-12C Financial Calculator

For those times when you don't have access to Excel, the program presented next can be entered into the HP-12C calculator and used to calculate the duration and modified duration of traditional fixed rate bonds. Enter the keystrokes for each step and confirm your progress with the information from the Display column.

Step	Keystrokes	Display
1	[f] [P/R]	
2	[f] [PRGM]	00-
3	[RCL] [FV]	01- 45 15
4	[STO] 2	02- 44 02
5	[RCL] [n]	03- 45 11
6	[x]	04- 20
7	[FV]	05- 15
8	[PV]	06- 13
9	[RCL] [n]	07- 45 11

Step	Keystrokes	Display
10	[CHS]	08- 16
11	[RCL] [PMT]	09- 45 14
12	[X]	10- 20
13	[FV]	11- 15
14	[PV]	12- 13
15	[RCL] [i]	13- 45 12
16	[/] *note: use divide key*	14- 10
17	1	15- 1
18	0	16- 0
19	0	17- 0
20	[STO] 1	18- 44 1
21	[x]	19- 20
22	[+]	20- 40
23	[RCL] 2	21- 45 2
24	FV	22- 15
25	PV	23- 13
26	[/] *note: use divide key*	24- 10
27	1	25- 1
28	[RCL] [i]	26- 45 12
29	[RCL] 1	27- 45 1
30	[/] *note: use divide key*	28- 10
31	[+]	29- 40
32	[/] *note: use divide key*	30- 10
33	f [P/R]	

OPERATING THE PROGRAM

1. Enter (or solve for) the # of payments and press [n]
2. Enter (or solve for) the bond's price and press [PV]
3. Enter (or solve for) the periodic payment and press [PMT]
4. Enter (or solve for) the bond's redemption value and press [FV]
5. Enter (or solve for) [i]
6. Press [R/S] to display modified duration in periods
7. Press [X><Y] to display duration in periods

information is not presented as a source of investment, tax, or legal advice. You should not rely on statements or representations made within the book or by any externally referenced sources. If you need investment, tax, or legal advice upon which you intend to rely in the course of your financial, business, or legal affairs, consult a competent, independent financial advisor, accountant, or attorney.

The contents of this book should not be taken as financial or legal advice, or as an offer to buy or sell any securities, fund, type of fund, or financial instruments. It should not be taken as an endorsement or recommendation of any particular company or individual, and no responsibility can be taken for inaccuracies, omissions, or errors. The information presented is not to be considered investment or legal advice. The reader should consult a Registered Investment Advisor or registered dealer or attorney prior to making any investment or legal decision.

The author does not assume any responsibility for actions or non-actions taken by people who have read this book, and no one shall be entitled to a claim for detrimental reliance based upon any information provided or expressed herein. Your use of any information provided herein does not constitute any type of contractual relationship between yourself and the provider(s) of this information. The author hereby disclaims all responsibility and liability for all use of any information provided in this book.

The materials here are not to be interpreted as establishing an attorney-client or any other relationship between the reader and the author or his firm.

Although great effort has been expended to ensure that only the most meaningful resources are referenced in these pages, the author does not endorse, guarantee, or warranty the accuracy, reliability, or thoroughness of any referenced information, product, or service. Any opinions, advice, statements, services, offers, or other information or content expressed or made available by third parties are those of the author(s) or publisher(s) alone. Reference to other sources of information does not constitute a referral, endorsement, or recommendation of any product or service. The existence of any particular reference is simply intended to imply potential interest to the reader.

The views expressed herein are exclusively those of the author and do not represent the views of any other person or any organization with which the author is, or may be, associated.

INDEX

Page numbers in **bold** indicate tables; those in *italics* indicate figures.

Stuart Veale is the president and founder of the Investment Performance Institute Inc., a firm that specializes in providing advanced-level practical capital markets training and consulting services to the financial services industry. Previously he was a senior vice president of portfolio strategy and design for the national sales group at Prudential Securities Inc. and senior vice president of advanced training at PaineWebber Inc.

Over the last 30 years, Mr. Veale has trained more than 6,000 capital markets professionals on portfolio design, trading strategies, risk analysis, derivative pricing and strategies, fixed income portfolio management, equity pricing and analysis, CFA I and II Prep, and numerous other securities-related topics. He has published six books: *The Handbook of the U.S. Capital Markets* (Harper Business), *Bond Yield Analysis* (New York Institute of Finance), *Tapping the Small Business Market* (New York Institute of Finance), *Essential Investment Math* (International Financial Press), *Essential Asset Allocation* (International Financial Press), and *Stocks, Bonds, Options, Futures* (Prentice Hall Press). He has also published numerous financial articles in magazines such as *Registered Representative*, *Cash Flow Magazine*, and *Medical Economics*.